GW00383039

"*The danger of Zen Centers or monasteries is
that people will take them seriously as being real.
We should find our own practice; we might start out
in an official place, but we should discover somehow
that we don't need official institutions. It's exactly
like Lew Welch says in his poem about
the rock out there, the Wobbly Rock. 'Somebody
showed it to me and I found it myself.'
...The real tension, I think, is between official poetry,
the kind that we're taught in school and is kept
in libraries, and the kind we really believe in—
what we are writing and what our friends write.
The same thing holds for meditation: what we
discover for ourselves and learn.
At some point you can forget it and go off
and make a pot of spaghetti.*"

•

Philip Whalen

from *Beneath a Single Moon:
Buddhism in Contemporary American Poetry*
Edited by Kent Johnson & Craig Paulenich
(Shambhala Publications)

Dirty Laundry

Dirty Laundry

100 Days in a Zen Monastery

Robert Winson

∞

Miriam Sagan

Afterword by Tom Ireland

NEW WORLD LIBRARY • NOVATO, CALIFORNIA

New World Library
14 Pamaron Way
Novato, California 94949

Copyright © 1997, 1999 by Miriam Sagan

Dirty Laundry was originally published by
La Alameda Press
9636 Guadalupe Trail NW
Albuquerque, New Mexico 87114

All rights reserved. No part of this book may be reproduced
in any form or by any means, including electronic or mechanical,
without the expressed consent of the publisher and author, with the
exception of brief passages in critical reviews or scholarship.

The original design for this book was done
by Suzanne Vilmain for *Fish Drum Press;*
J. B. Bryan extended her text concept
for *La Alameda Press.*

Cover photograph: Russell Lee
(detail) *Washday—Chamisal, New Mexico*
Farm Security Administration Project, 1940
negative # LC-USF 33-12820-M4

Library of Congress Cataloging-in-Publication Data available
First printing, November 1999
ISBN 1-57731-105-1
Printed in Canada on acid-free paper
Distributed to the trade by Publishers Group West
10 9 8 7 6 5 4 3 2 1

Him: Robert ◎ Her: Miriam

Dirty Laundry: 100 Days in a Zen Monastery was a collaborative diary, written by a husband and wife over a four-month period. It is a complex document, both personally and structurally. Five years ago, my husband Robert Winson, who was also an ordained monk in the Soto Zen lineage of Buddhism, decided to spend a practice period in a remote monastery in Crestone, Colorado, in the Sangre de Cristo Mountains. I was a thirty-seven-year-old wife and mother, poet and teacher. Robert was thirty-two, a library worker, rock-and-roller, and small press publisher. We had a daughter, Isabel, almost three years old. In large part because we felt Isabel should not be parted from Robert for too long, we set up a commuting situation where I would drive every week or so between Santa Fe, New Mexico, and the monastery—a distance of about two hundred miles, often in rough winter weather.

It was my idea that we have a project together, a joint diary. We each began our own private journal the day we left for Crestone. Our method was to write whatever we wanted, then edit it for each other's consumption. At one point in the diary I gave us a shared topic—the topic of anger. This resulted in several pages of introspective lists.

The diary began as an innocent record. Robert recorded monastic life, I domestic. Tensions grew. We found the monastic life and community difficult, at times impossibly in contradiction to family life. We quarreled, we fretted. Midway through, Robert decided to leave his original Zen teacher. In Zen, a monk who does this is "nine-fingered" for having cut off an essential digit.

The diary was unintentionally a record of dissatisfaction and disillusionment. It is also the record of a man who was sicker than he realized. Robert was diagnosed at the time as having ulcerative colitis. Four years later, he died in Albuquerque's Presbyterian Hospital of the aftereffects of surgery meant to cure him. It is haunting to read now of his stoical endurance of pain and blood, and wonder at the prescience of his death imagery.

The diary also chronicles parents' fascination with and love for a child. We shared one smallish room, living in it together as if we were nomads in a tent. The difficult details of taking care of our daughter in a monastery comes through as undercurrent, if not whirlpool.

For me, the diary also was prescient. Richard Feldman, mentioned in one passage, came back into my life as a partner after Robert's death. Robert teased me for the phrase "the past is heating up," but it was, in ways I never imagined.

After the hundred days had passed, we gave each other our barely censored versions. Robert planned to publish it under his Fish Drum Press. We took out harmful gossip where we could. The troubles and peccadilloes of friends and family members were a leitmotiv to what we experienced ourselves, but people have been disguised or had their names changed. We left the monastic setting pretty much unchanged. Readers may find ideas here about American Buddhism—a critique of community or the student/teacher relationship—but for Robert it was mostly a simple and honest observation of a world he loved and was committed to.

Robert Winson never wanted to be anything but a Zen priest. His ordination name was Sei Gen Yo San. The first part refers to a lineage teacher; the second means something like "willow tree by a blue/green watercourse." When he died, a group of friends, family, and Buddhist practitioners chanted the Heart Sutra in the intensive care unit. He was cremated in a traditional fashion. At a memorial service a year later, many offered incense in his memory.

Robert really loved almost everything in the diaries—Buddhism, landscape, sex, food, trashy reading, being a monk, being a father. This book is dedicated to his memory:

Robert Winson • Sei Gen Yo San • 1959–1995
~Gassho~

Miriam Sagan
October, 1996 :: Santa Fe, New Mexico
Sunday :: Snowstorm

Dirty Laundry

100 Days

Him

Woke up with a song: "The ants go marching one by one, hurrah, hurrah... And they all go marching, down into the ground to get out of the rain, boom boom."

Many loose ends remaining before we leave, and I have an agreement with Miriam to leave at a specific time, rather than run errands all day and drive in the dark as we usually do. I pack everything that looks like it might be useful—mostly warm clothes—nothing to continue my home life except Miriam and Isabel.

Two calls come in, one from the monastery. With the extra errands we're only an hour late. Miriam is sour and grumpy for much of the trip. We're nearly there before I learn that she's not resentful or having traveling anxiety, but is in pain from her nearly gone bronchitis and maybe the missing lobe of her lung. Isabel rides cheerfully in back of the tiny Toyota with the boxes and baggage. Except for a few brief tantrums, mostly demands for freedom, she's content to demand stories.

1.1.92
DATE

Miriam improvises some more episodes of the "Princess of Tangles," and we sing some songs. Miriam and I remember ones from childhood with the same choruses and different verses. Mine went, "The teacher died and that was the end of school." Sang "Yellow Submarine." Isabel wants explanations for everything. "WHY do we have to be quiet in a monastery?" She's satisfied for a while with, "so we can see what we feel like inside."

Hard to quiet Isabel down. We arrange our room, call Abbie (my mother) to wish her happy birthday, wander in and out of the kitchen, and I read to her from *Indian Tales,* ending the day's adventure with good-nights to the objects in the room.

Her

Two things I hate—going to a monastery and starting a diary.

Long drive up—first the familiar—the opera, Camel Rock, Pojoaque, turn at Española, turn at the round windowless adobe building for Ojo Caliente, a surprising view of San Antonio Mountain, that large lump of sugarcoated oatmeal, where steers are tiny specks on the slope. Diner and store closed tight in Tres Piedras, then Antonito, Alamosa. Going north the Sangre de Cristos are a huge breakable snowcapped white wave on my right-hand side. It's dusk when we arrive.

My lung hurts along the scar, adhesions or fear when I sneeze or cough. Robert is an hour late packing and then runs errands, including grocery shopping for the monastery. I resent how much he doesn't take me into consideration. Still, we don't fight.

1.1.92
DATE

Him

Isabel was up all night. Heater flooding the room with heat, window cracked open bitterly cold.

The beginning of the schedule was sweet, morning *zazen* (sitting meditation) at the center of the world. Familiar ceremony: seating ourselves in the candlelight, robe chant, zazen, *kinhin* (walking meditation), zazen, service (chanting and bowing), has some additional power and feeling of inevitability in a group this large, in a place this isolated. Mopped the kitchen and set the breakfast table for *soji* (silent cleaning). I've learned, slowly, to survive a semiformal meal without suffering too much, by sitting quietly and being alert.

1.2.92
DATE

Isabel and I took a long bath. I shaved my head in a leisurely way. We had a long conversation about who shaves their heads and why—"Do little girls shave their heads?" (hardly ever)—who was at my ordination, breaking rocks, and what is jail. Isabel spent much time tenderly caring for her shampoo bottle, which has a doll head, wrapping it up in a washcloth and cradling it in her arms.

Her

Night from hell—Isabel shrieking awake every few hours—heater too hot, Robert and I thrashing; he has colitis, my lung hurts. We're all in one room, two beds, a rocking chair, table, tree stump, no reading lamp. Stone walls still have their lichen. Huge vigas. Bells and wooden *han* (sounding board) for zazen. Robert gets up. In the morning he looks jovial, goofy, and slightly whiskered. Baker-roshi tells me: you are a good sport to put up with all this. He wears a robe of gold cloth; I wear a pair of pajamas with a rose print, $24.99 from Lerner's in the mall. Our usual friends aren't here yet; mostly there are the German students. C. has cancer. Gisela was just ordained. Gisela and Ulrike hug me. Gerald acts slightly weird, as if he has no idea who I am.

Up at 7:30 A.M., bath with Isabel. She tells Baker-roshi: the dark is gone and the sun is here. There's a lot of snow outside our window. Start work on the revision of my novel—I've got it—feels completely clear— adding a whole new level—the killer speaks, the childless woman.

1.2.92
DATE

Robert sits and reads *Indian Tales* to Isabel, who looks mesmerized. She's not settled in, refusing to pee in her potty, drinking a lot of bottles, acting cranky baby. She locked herself into our room during formal breakfast, could not be cajoled out, but luckily we found a key.

Him

The regular crew, the half-dozen people who really run the place, are all gone, and the jobs have been handed off. I'm *doan* (on bells, drum, and sounding board) until they get back; only they've added several other jobs to it without telling me. The batteries failed this morning before 5, and I rummaged for shoes, coat, hat in the dark before charging outside with the wake-up bell to start the day for the guys in the woodshop. Stilled the bell to open Roshi's door and call up the stairs when his voice came out of a door to the left. Ulrike's room? We began the day ten minutes late. During *sesshin* (weeklong meditation) that kind of thing could set the tone for a whole day, but I'm happy to be here. I feel in place.

1.3.92
DATE

Helping in the kitchen with Isabel, who spends an hour washing and arranging zucchini. When she gets bored I find her a cake and a glass of milk. It's fun, but very wearing to keep an eye on her while doing something else. Puts housework in a different light; so much of it can be done while minding children. Roshi says, "The skills of a monk are the skills of a housewife." I sew up a rip in Curious George's back.

I've been reading to Isabel from Jaime D'Angulo's *Indian Tales,* which have her mesmerized. Miriam and I talked about it last night, after she was asleep. She seems to be at a stage where narrative and meaning are the same thing; she can't possibly understand all the details of the tales, interiors of Indian longhouses, etc., but she doesn't care as long as it keeps moving. If you slow too much, she says in a hard voice, "Tell the Story!" And she remembers the details, saying today that Weasel burned the world because he was angry, and that he doesn't like people, which was from yesterday's reading. She's visualizing it, too: the part where the crows are making fire come up out of the ground by screaming over a hole scared her. While we were talking, Isabel rose out of sleep and demanded something: I thought she said "needles," but Miriam, with the insight of a parent who's heard something a thousand times, heard "Princess of Tangles."

Her

Dream that X. has a baby boy whom she ignores. She is distraught over her infertility and attempting to conceive another child. Talks to her husband, who says she is crazy.

Wake up to a strange rhythmic pounding. At first I decide it is an enormous woodpecker, then a malfunctioning generator. Only as I wake up do I recognize it for what it is—the drum for morning service.

Robert says he likes tempeh.

I say I hate tempeh.

I say: we must be writing pretty different things in our journals.

I am thirty-seven years old.

Robert is thirty-two.

Isabel is almost three.

1.3.92
DATE

Huge fat-fronted robin redbreast sitting on the snowy picnic table outside the window. I clean up the room. Isabel says, "You're good at this, and it's a hard job." She arranges her many tiny plastic babies on the wood stump that serves as a kind of table. A plastic polar bear, and a panda, too. Robert says: living in a monastery with a baby is as logistically complicated as living on the street—how to eat, where to take a shower—it takes up all your time. Isabel breathes heavily as she concentrates. Babies in a ring.

Breakfast is vastly irritating—we don't eat a formal meal with the students. No one seems to actually get this. No one puts out a bowl for us. I feel like an intrusive idiot just trying to get two bowls of cereal. And by 9 A.M. still have got no coffee.

Dry grass poking through snow. A dog the color of orange pekoe tea. Picnic table under three separate weights of snow, like picnickers and picnic. Isabel in her neon pink and orange jacket climbing on the Noguchi statue called ZAZEN.

Ralph—tall black guy—lectures on Vipassana. He was an army brat in Japan. His family were ministers in a church on an island off North Carolina. In Japan he studied martial arts. The first day he went to the dojo he saw a man sitting cross-legged in midair. His teacher piled up bricks so high he had to stand on a stepladder to break the stack. Ralph cleaned them up. One brick was left. Ralph hit it with his hand and almost landed in the hospital.

1.3.92
DATE

Him

Steve and Angelique came in last night from San Francisco. I threw myself on them. When Miriam came in she did the same. Isabel was intrigued to hear that Angel'd peered in at her when she was a tiny baby in a crib. It changes the atmosphere of this floaty interim schedule to have two more monks around. Besides, these two I trust; we have a lot of history in common, San Francisco Zen Center to Santa Fe to here, and I can let my hair down with them, which Angel and I did 'til late last night.

Today is *shikunichi*, a "4 and 9" day, with no schedule after breakfast. Isabel isn't acclimating to this very adult environment too well—she's having tantrums, getting up a lot at night; acting about six months younger. Miriam says being in one room with us isn't good for her. I'm not sure that's true. It's a big number in this culture: separating the infant, the child's room. What is true is that it's hard on us, waking with every cry. I went off to heat some water, light a fire in the *zendo* (meditation hall), fire up the altar, hit the han for fifteen minutes before zazen, sat, was doan for service, cleaned, and came in before breakfast to find Miriam already fried to a crisp. I took Isabel for a while before breakfast, then to noon. Miriam slept. Isabel and I escorted some visitors around for an hour, having tea and walking outside.

1.4.92
DATE

Did handwash.

Roshi introduced me to the visitors as a sometime writer, and I told him later I didn't mind being presented as a Zen student.

Hurriedly made dinner with Petra, a German guest student. Isabel helped me carry a box of linguine and chop some oranges.

Someone fielded a call during dinner—they let the phone ring loud and always answer. Steve and Roshi and all the officers being gone, it got handed to me.

Watched *Harold and Maude* in the kitchen for warmth.

The energetic, brusque way Roshi moves his hands at table: as if he's aware of the conventions, or of his own past precise formalities, and is operating those large hands outside them by moving large amounts of his body energy with them. It's oddly brutal and direct. I mention this to Miriam, who says, "he needs more exercise."

Dream: shopping with Russell in an antique, or expensive junk, shop. They don't have what we want: a phonograph player incorporating a cat. Diane appears in the dream.

Her

1.4.92
DATE

Snow in the morning and snow in the afternoon. Isabel up half the night. She seems to know we are constrained here. Nap in the morning, more novel, etc. Angelique and Steve arrived last night. Angel whispers that she has two and a half cases of wine. She says she can survive here if she has her little things in order, like toothpicks and smoking two cigarettes a day. I tell her I must have hard candies, and do daily hand-wash.

Isabel gives Roshi her three baby dolls. He wears a long rose-colored wool overcoat. One of the babies has pink hair. Isabel tells him the plot of the Disney *Cinderella*.

Robert says I am a good sport, and what other wife would do this. In the middle of the night though I think: I hate Zen, I hate my husband, I hate being a mother, and I hate to write.

Running clouds in a blue sky.

Four day monastic day off.

I wrote a wretched entry in this diary this morning, but I threw it out.

Angel says that she grew her hair out because when she was ordained every lesbian in San Francisco chased her and her shaved head. She also says that Kathy Acker has a black panther tattooed on her butt. Angel's ex is Kathy's current boyfriend.

Roshi is happy. Robert is totally happy. I wear my bright stretch pants. No mail.

Him

Fought with Miriam about money, which colored much of the day. Wasn't a very out-there fight, but it's a direct result of the pressure of being here, and I had that sour, angry-sleepy resentful distance on the day, and napped with Isabel in the afternoon. Mark is back from working Xmas at Gardenswartz Sports in Albuquerque, and lunch showed his hand as *tenzo* (head cook): simple, efficient, tasty, with cookies. Isabel and I worked in the morning. She washed carrots; I grated them and cut cabbage, added olives, dressing.

I can hear Mark and Lynne doing crossword puzzles through the wall. We're moving back into a regular, noninterim schedule, so there is an afternoon work period and an extra period of evening zazen. I'll ask Mark to be doan so I can sit with Isabel and Miriam can go to the zendo.

Mark and I were jokingly trying out our German on Petra: "kindergarten," "gesundheit," "poltergeist." Mark says, "Jawohl, Herr Kommandant," which is a joke for me; the Europeans have had trouble believing there was ever a television comedy like *Hogan's Heroes*.

Petra says that not only has she never baked cookies, she's never followed a recipe. Miriam says she thinks there are a lot of class distinctions among the Germans we're not getting. Ulrike says at lunch, apropos of Ralph having got a Purple Heart, that the Germans gave a medal to women who had ten children. S. says, "That was the Nazis, I think," the only time I've ever heard any of the Germans mention them voluntarily.

It's hard feeling disconnected from Miriam. My most comfortable state is physical closeness with some head privacy. She actually is relationally trustworthy; I just react violently when she talks like she isn't, saying today, "This relationship is ending anyway; I figure it'll be over about April." Then, of course, she's upset that I'm cold.

Isabel: "I want to tell you something. When I was Mom I rang the bell, I sat on the cushion I sat zazen. When I was Fox Boy I had the HA-HA's. When I was Coyote Old Man I was careful. When I was Oriole I was black and orange. You know what? I talked to Isabel and I told her I liked bad witches."

Her

Fight with Robert about money in the A.M. and get depressed. Go back to bed. Worry what is wrong with me. PMS.

Much better night with Isabel. She woke up once. Turn on lights, wake her fully. Help her out of that in-between state. She doesn't like it, but it works.

Roshi lies down in the snow and prints a six-foot snow angel for Isabel. She is funny and sweet all day. Wake up, bath and breakfast. We draw and write. She and Robert "work" in the kitchen. Lunch, a walk, quiet play, a nap. She plays with her elves-in-a-bag. I make one ride her polar bear.

No novel, read editing manuscript, poem, book, journal, letter, phone calls, wash. I feel introverted and eat star-shaped anise cookies.

I should stop reevaluating everything every fifteen minutes.

Him

Last night Isabel and I bundled up and walked out while Miriam was in last period zazen, and looked at the stars and the lights of Roshi's octagonal tower room. Isabel: "Are you playing, stars? They can't talk to us." When I read to her: "The letters are falling off the page."

Cooked breakfast this morning with Angelique: garlicky scrambled eggs, biscuits, peach tea.

Miriam and I straightened out the money thing.

Beautiful Brazilian woman showed up at the door with small child and stuck car. What is she doing here in the outback? Coming to see Gisela, of course. She's the wife of a dentist in Moffat. I told Mark that if I was good, Miriam would give her to me. Played with Isabel and visiting child Kim.

1.6.92
DATE

Intestines destroyed by too much curried lunch.

Read to Isabel for hours.

Read for myself some in *The Eastern Buddhist* and *CQ*.

Her

Zazen last night, coughing fit, nausea, pins and needles, tunnel vision, the usual. A vivid hallucination of that clamshell I saw open in the moonlight at Foxes' Bottom Beach, maybe 1959.

Robert took Isabel out with a flashlight to look at the stars.

Isabel has fits until 11 P.M., tantrum, no sleeping. She was upset about peeing in the bed. Her toilet-training consciousness is up, but seems stressful. I did my tough love routine and she slept until 8 A.M., waking only once, and being good about it.

Snow, then sun. A little girl shows up, Kim, eighteen months. Her mother is a gorgeous Brazilian named Z. who is married to the dentist in Moffat. America is an unbelievable place. Z. has two other daughters, ages eight and four. She is lovely and exotic, skinny with masses of black hair. She says she is not good at driving on snow.

1.6.92
DATE

We resolve our fight with the monastery about money. They give us a slightly reduced rate, but not as much as we want. This relieves me of any residual guilt around not working for the community here. I'm angry, not about the sum of $100 but because they told us ten different things at different times. It makes me feel ungenerous.

Him

Angelique is ill so I dragoon Mark as assistant cook. Pancakes and cottage cheese, bananas, condiments, tea, coffee. Roshi compliments it (saying also that fluffy pancakes are decadent), and addresses his comments to Mark, though Mark points out that I'm the cook. Angelique says, "If he doesn't feel you're committed to him, he doesn't empower you."

Go to work meeting and announce again that I'll do in the kitchen what Isabel will. However, Lynne takes her much of the morning and afternoon as well while she sews winter robes for Gerald. Isabel seems delighted to be shut of us—she won't let me in the room when I come to check that Lynne is okay. Lynne made her a gold paper ring with a red square "stone" of paper.

I visit with Roshi in the two facing chairs at the foot of his bed. His room is even more crowded with rich chachtkas, books, computer, magazines, art, than before, if possible. S. called it (and Roshi repeated at table) "a room out of control." I tell him what I've been doing, settling in here.

I.7.92
DATE

He asked me how old I am. I said thirty-three, hoping that was right—birthday in a few months, turning thirty-three? thirty-four? He: "When I was two years older I was abbot of Zen Center." I'm embarrassed—like hearing, "When Mozart was your age he'd been dead for two years." Having been yelled at in this very seat for being frivolous and "shining things off," I don't say anything.

There's going to be a seminar for people who're going to teach. He doesn't want people who just want not to be excluded. "We should exclude them until they no longer mind." He wants us to ask questions that come entirely from us—"The kinds of questions I asked Suzuki-roshi: every major question of Buddhism. I badgered him until he told me."

I say that since I was ordained I've felt there was a problem in that I wasn't close to him.

Spend a gossipy hour with Ulrike and Angelique, who're smoking, and Ulrike's ex-husband David, who's sewing his *rakusu* (lay initiate's cloth). Ulrike describes a book on her shelves, a psychology of why people become priests: "people who are rebels but not strong enough to live outside of society like artists." Angel and I bridle. David points out that structure is offered to Christian clergy in a way it isn't to American Zen people.

Talk with Miriam and Steve at dinner about asking questions. Miriam says that she prefers, when poets come to her for help, not to be told how terrible they are, not to be asked to make things all right but, "Here, the beginning is okay but there's something wrong with this part." Steve says that the student needs to come forward and be seen, to show both themselves and their ignorance.

Her

Zazen last night. Thirty minutes of warm body feeling and ten minutes of panic hell.

Come back to the room and had a nice chat with Robert and a sweet, slightly guilty fuck under the sheets, hot and silent. Isabel woke a bit in the night, but no tantrums.

Mark was married once to a woman named Bianca Martinez up in Cuba.

Ulrike and I confess to each other that we like to do laundry.

Finger-paint with Isabel, who looks at Mother Goose book by herself. She plays at length in Lynne's room. Kitty chases a Ping-Pong ball.

What is objective, what is subjective, what is narrative.

Objective: it snowed last night.

Subjective: after a few days here this life seems real, and it's hard to deal with the phone messages.

Narrative: Ulrike used to be married to David, now she is Roshi's girlfriend. The three of them sit together at the table, David and Ulrike almost touching. David is very unhappy and doesn't know it.

1.7.92
DATE

Him

Make, for lack of a better idea, a "traditional" three-bowl monastic breakfast: seven-grain cereal, tofu scrambler, yogurt, adding condiments and milk. Roshi compliments the food to me.

Miriam and Isabel leave today—Roshi passes me in the hall and says, "He's just a lonely boy." But I'm not; I'm enjoying the day as a monastic one, working on cutting Roshi's robe hangers to fit the closet and shoveling snow to make a walkway to Don's cabin for his return.

We have a two-and-a-half-hour seminar in the afternoon on case #70 in the *Shoyoroku*. They've been at it four weeks. It's opaque to me, but I find an entry. Steve says something brilliant that shows me the territory of the koan. I don't remember him being this lucid. Roshi lambastes us at the end: "It's possible that you're inadequate; but it's more likely that I am.... My job is to arouse your Way-seeking mind. That's all." He asked about the line in Jiaofan's poem, "Time after time seeds produce manifest patterns"—why no one knew what that referred to. Steve said "bijas" [Sanskrit: seeds]. I said, seeds, as in the *alaya-vijnana*. The group was resistant. Roshi was more forceful than he usually is in public—I was exhausted by the end. Philip has a poem that says, "The development of insight consumes great quantities of protein."

1.8.92
DATE

Her

Good period of zazen last night, following Robert's advice to use my breath to create posture.

Gorgeous sun on snow this morning. Mark makes a trail with the Trooper and we follow him down the mountain. Stop briefly in Tres Piedras. Car heat gauge registers cold until Ojo Caliente. Stop and check fluids, which are fine. It is bitterly cold outside. Registers normal by Española. Fear of breaking down, fear of snow, slush, ice, trucks, mountains, dogs.

Arrive home safely, thanks to Virgin of Guadalupe gearshift knob prayers. Home seems luxurious, and not too overwhelming. It's clean and tidy, thanks to housesitter Joe. The monastery starts to fade immediately—the sense of being both crowded and stretched—but I'm suddenly lonely for Robert. Five minutes after we leave Isabel says: "I miss my daddy *already*."

1.8.92
DATE

Call Kaune's and have groceries delivered (my mother is still treating) and break out videos (also from grandma)—*Babar, Winnie-the-Pooh, Mouse on a Motorcycle.* Isabel is entranced by so many favorites and I get to land. Lovely to talk to Hope.

Am I happier at home? Yes, but more worried too. Yes, but for missing Robert.

Him

Shikunichi (monastic day off).

I make breakfast: grapefruit, crackers with melted Swiss, eggs with onions and mushrooms.

Just as I'm on top of things, the jobs are turning over.

Spend a couple hours in the kitchen talking to Steve and Angelique.

Philip's in the hospital with a piece of meat in his esophagus above the stomach where nothing, apparently, should be able to lodge. He's in the emergency room with tubes, one of them for food. They can't find the obstruction and are worried about why it's there, may operate. He's not in much pain. We're worried. I don't want the old man to die on me. I talked to him on the phone a couple days ago, asked him how he was doing. He said, "Don't WORRY." "I'm not worrying." "NO, YOU'RE TENSE!"

1.9.92
DATE I have a headache and nap around noon, then get some aspirin from Lynne and take a long bath in the afternoon.

Dennis is wandering around with that sun-blasted look that crazies get, on the street or not. He asks me what time it is. I look at him. The clock is right behind him. He says, "I don't know why, but I don't want to look at the clock right now."

Her

Santa Fe looks spectacular after the monastery.

First day out—

Buy meat, red wine,

Pink hyacinth

Also—chocolate cookies.

Robert calls to say Philip Whalen is sick, in the hospital. A piece of meat lodged mysteriously outside his esophagus.

Isabel sits in the bathtub and says: my daddy is dead. Last night I pasted up two pictures of him in her room.

Mail, phone calls, bills, listen to *Poetry Devils*, sell clothes, library, Isabel to and from day care, shop, cook stew, listen to Robert Browning tape, wait for mail, Miriam Bobkoff drops by. Poetry reading at the synagogue tonight, wear brilliant flowered tights and black wedge dress, colored crystal earrings.

1.9.92
DATE

Isabel pees in the potty all afternoon.

The amaryllis and lilies of the valley will bloom in their pots, but will I be here?

Him

Many college students in the zendo in the A.M. make waves I can feel. Someone nabs my *zafu* (meditation cushion), which throws my posture out of whack.

Instead of soji, we have tea in the kitchen, the only warm room; instead of chatting with a student, Ulrike and I talk by the sink. She says Miriam's notion that there are class distinctions among the German Zen students that're invisible to us is quite true, and that she's lower middle class, which surprises me. Her great-grandfather was a fisherman. Roshi reaches pointedly between us to leave his teacup. She tells me about going to Elba with him.

Roshi chastises Lynne, Mark, and myself for serving the three students who stayed a too-weird, too-formal silent meal (tofu scrambler, miso soup, and oatmeal without milk). I had nothing to do with it, but don't say anything.

1.10.92
DATE

Afternoon off. Put away some leftover dishes. Study the intro to the *Shoyoroku,* which has an interesting rundown of analytical Zen constructs: the five ranks, etc. Eat pretzels with Angel and discuss the hierarchy—she says Gerald is mean and playing dominance games. Read until dinner. Dennis made delicious stuffed onions.

Luxury of a private room—sitting in it makes me realize how dinky the arrangement of Isabel's drawings and the too-small framed paintings is—I'll leave them alone.

Two periods evening zazen—replacement cushion all wrong.

Her

Reading was a great success at the synagogue last night—about 200 people—parking all the way down the street as if it were Yom Kippur.

Got my period.

Guy in truck scraped Toyota and took a fingernail-sized chunk out of the right rear light.

Advance copy of my novel *Coastal Lives* arrives. It is gorgeous! I love it. Feel purely happy. It is a book!

Philip out of ICU.

Reading *The Dead Girl.*

Why am I always backlogged with other peoples' manuscripts, poems, notes, paper, pleas, messages, etc.

Waxing moon.

A friendly sparrow.

Dialogue with Isabel:

Me: We're going to Monica's.

Isabel: Where's Joe?

Me: Monica and Joe had a fight and don't live together anymore.

Isabel: You and daddy have a fight.

Me: Yes we do, but we love each other and kiss and make up.

Isabel: You and me have a fight.

Me: Yes, but we shake and make up.

Isabel: Where's Joe?

Me: Monica needs a new boyfriend.

Isabel: If Reuben and I fight, I would need a new boyfriend.

Me: Who is your new boyfriend?

Isabel: You are, mom.

Him

Dreamed that I'd just realized the problem with my life was that I needed a girlfriend, and that Brian was out of the band and I was trying to put together another.

This morning Steve's wearing his brown robes, signifying dharma transmission. His are flat dark brown, Philip's are bright gold. Funny how a word covers a multitude of realities.

DECISIONS ARE MADE:

Miriam had trouble with Gerald last year over the washing machine. Using it requires that the generator be on, and Gerald wasn't willing to let her use it, two-year-old child or no. This year I carefully explained in advance to Randy, the director, that what we needed was lots of access to the washing machine. He okayed it. When we got there, he said use it whenever you want, no one seems to be using it since the old year's washing schedule lapsed; they're washing their clothes in Crestone or Alamosa 'cause it takes too long for them to dry here. Came up in work meeting this morning that the lapse was due to a blocked water pipe, which Gerald fixed without telling anyone that the machine was now working. People had been doing handwash (Randy said they *preferred* doing handwash). Mark made a schedule that didn't include Miriam or Isabel. I had to slowly convince him of infant need, glad the whole time that Miriam wasn't here to witness.

Steve led a long, fairly intense seminar that was supposed to be on case #70. Dennis attacked: "How do you defend this," etc. I suspect lineage doesn't mean much to them. They're fixated on Roshi—assume you can't learn from anyone else.

Steve talked about the kind of crisis we were in, engendered by living in a monastery, whose structure reflects your hindrances back at you. I remember vividly all my years of resistance to these seminars: claustrophobia, pulling back, doodling on the page, never looking up, passive, not speaking to the point.

Her

Snow.

Fire in fireplace.

Children's Museum with Reuben, Hope. Hope's sister-in-law, with three daughters under the age of four, is off from Shiprock temporarily, but goes back in the snow, four hours across empty reservation.

Dream that neither Lewis nor David Cuneo is a suitable boyfriend, and so fuck some skinny guy who likes me. Robert leaves a message on the machine in real life: come back soon. I dreamed I needed a new girlfriend.

1.11.92
DATE

Him

Gerald reminded me during soji that the Suzuki-roshi altar's incense bowl needs to be cleaned. Yesterday he told me after soji, and so I left it for today, feeling a little annoyed and a little guilty. Today I'd already done it. He added that Roshi wants us to be in the zendo five minutes before the beginning of zazen, or we should sit in the atrium, then said people often get mad at him for telling them this. I was angry at him, for his manner and for his insistence on extending work periods, but not for what he was just then softly pointing out.

Called Isabel on the phone before breakfast, figuring she'd be getting ready for school. She told me she missed me, sounding very articulate. Said she'd gone to the museum with Reuben and his boy and girl brothers (i.e., cousins) and Hope, but Greg had to stay at work all alone. Also that she was coming to see us soon, that then we were never never never going home, mama had said so, and so she was sad. Miriam got on the phone and said that was a misunderstanding, and they kiss my picture goodnight every night.

1.12.92
DATE

> At breakfast Mark asks, "How is Gisela?"
> Gerald says shortly, "She's better."
> "What does she have?" asks Randy.
> "Maybe you'd better ask her," says Gerald.

> Gerald: "We resolve our conflicts in the zendo."
> Miriam: "They're afraid of words, of speaking."
> Wu-men: "To cultivate samadhi meditation is to practice in a haunted house."

Cut my head all over shaving for the ceremony this evening. Took a big flap off the top of my forehead. A too-worn razor, though I enjoy getting as much use as possible out of them. Inhibitions against wasting.

Lovely lay ordination ceremony for David. He hesitated at the sixth precept, "no sexual misconduct."

Her

Run around all day doing errands, buy a poncho for Petra in the monastery, Isabel's birthday presents, garbage can. Isabel is a reasonable child all day and goes without diapers successfully for eight hours. I buy her five tiny baby dolls, which are a big hit.

Lots of snow in the afternoon. I'm surprised at how easy this weekend was with Isabel, but we feel synchronized.

Things that help:
    a clean house
    video
    spending money
    not trying to do too much
    laughing
    letting well enough alone
    flowers
    proper shoes
    a book
    getting off the phone
    knowing Robert loves me
    everything changes

1.12.92
DATE

Him

Dokusan (interview) with Roshi this morning:

Mark gives Petra orders about the grain mill, and when finally he turns to leave, all the English-speaking Germans in the room say, "Ja-wohl, Herr Kommandant."

Gerald calls a doan meeting, which maunders endlessly. He says nothing until the end, then: "I don't mind all this discussion if we practice the doan work."

Angel, Lynne, and I stay up 'til ten talking about crazies we've known, including Angel's mother and James: both of them street people. James was lovers with Angel's mother and her teacher Issan as well. James kicked the door in at Hartford St. Zen Center, beat up Issan, probably gave him AIDS, roller-skated to Tassajara Monastery, lived in a hole on the beach. Lynne said they've only had one up here, an alcoholic. They persuaded the liquor store owner not to sell to her, but he ended up drinking with her, giving her booze. Thinking she was passed out in the atrium they went to make up a room for her, then found her in the kitchen, standing on the table waving a knife with blood running down her arm. "I was trying to make a sandwich," she said.

1.13.92
DATE

Her

Snow. Very tired.

Him

Shikunichi. One period zazen, short service. Good chanting. Lynne makes breakfast. I nap from nine to noon, waking for a couple knocks on the door, including Roshi. Shower, talk to Petra for a while, transcribe some more Roshi lecture on his old typewriter.

Slow, sunny day. Bright snow-sun outside.

My intestines are acting up again—bleeding a little. We're all farting wildly. Diet.

Watched *Hunt for Red October,* which I'd already seen on the Vineyard with Miriam. Audience of four Americans, three Germans, one British.

Her

Yesterday I realized quite suddenly that I won't have another child.

Tuesday writing group—"edit femmes"—nice to use my brain.

Isabel goes to Cory's for lunch—big girl!

Dream of rabbis, and a globe made out of playdough, or Renée's necklace.

Fir tree weighted under snow.

Patti Smith in Paris. Why is she so much better than me, or Algebra Suicide?

Why am I the only person in this town who does not believe—profoundly—that the mind can alter the body, that the mind heals?

I believe the body heals.

I also believe that the body does not, ultimately, heal.

Snow White and the Evil Queen—
Menstrual stain—

1.14.92
DATE

Bleeding thumb—
My only daughter
Dances in the snow.

Isabel has a nightmare about me and won't tell me what it is.

Him

Stayed up too late reading last night. Tired through zazeh (came in just after second rolldown on the han). Swept and shoveled outside, cleaned off the solar panels for soji. COLD, my fingers bitten in their thick mittens.

Odds and ends for work period. Helped Gerald lift a kitchen cabinet over a pipe in his still-building house. Helped Don move a gas refrigerator he was fixing. Read the Bookpeople catalog in my room.

1.15.92
DATE

Talking about Roshi's fax and laser printer and phone lines at lunch. Ulrike was joking that if someone sent a fax transmission when he was listening on the phone line the paper'd come out of his mouth. Last week she was planning to make an ashtray out of his skull.

Doan practice in the afternoon and another page of transcription. Tape recorder is breaking down. Did some childproofing: removed kerosene lamp oil, Drano, detergent, bleach from floor and low shelves. Found two child-size red metal chairs.

Very cold in common spaces of the house—too cold to do more than pass through. Room is overheated.

Gisela: "Do you think we could ask Steve to be shorter? It goes on too long. I get tired listening to him. I don't get tired listening to Roshi, but I get tired listening to Steve. I have to think about it too much. It's too hard."

Her

Hope and Reuben gave Isabel a tiny beautiful tea set—Mexican pottery from Jackalope. She loves it!

Tea party with Maggie and Susan. Teach private lesson. Depressing snow in the morning. Buy Isabel an incredible cake for her school birthday party tomorrow: Little Mermaid in a blue sea of waves. Get her hair trimmed. I love her so much. She says, "I like your writing," and watches *Mary Poppins*. I feel like a good mother—bake cookies, buy batteries. Everyone says the house feels good—femmy-girl space. Keep it all going.

Home: cans of soup, telephone, potted bulbs, drying rack.

Monastery: one room, snow, and monks, no housework, handwash on drying rack.

1.15.92
DATE

Him

Dokusan.

I: "Muuuu..."

Roshi: "It's not like a cartoon bubble coming out of the mouth of a cartoon character...it should be out in the world. When you chant the *eko* (dedication of merit), it should be all one breath... Muuu... Muuu... Muuu... (rising and falling, continuous). I've noticed that you're brighter. Not smarter, but more responsive, less in your body." He qualified the "out of body" part, meaning in a good way.

Miriam says she heard Isabel telling Reuben that she was tired now, and was going to the monastery to rest and see her friends.

Writing to Philip yesterday I complained that the conversation here is usually rather guarded and flat, and that the other basics of life are also pinched—anxiety about food, money, short supplies of water, heat, electricity.

Walking with the old man in Chinatown
He's grown sweet in his blindness
Misremembering our way
Past fishmarket alleys to Giant Dim Sum

Her

Carry 750 copies of *Coastal Lives* into the house, and can feel all that labor in my body, every copy.

Thursday P.M., first class, goes well, editing and writing. Stay up until 11:30 P.M. talking with Kath about death. She looks beautiful and dark.

1.16.92
DATE

Him

I'm irritable. Have been since yesterday—a slight slacking off from the do-the-next-thing engagement of the past couple weeks. Evening and morning zazen full of thoughts of how annoyed I am. Not sure why, really, and it's a diffuse feeling. There's a physical component to this: feeling nervous and unsettled yesterday afternoon when Roshi was being brilliant for those college kids.

Miriam and Isabel are coming today, and I tend to squabble with her around comings and goings—must be careful, do one thing at a time.

Philip: smooth-skinned reassuring old man. Motherly. Cranky. Philip is an OBJECT. Large, soft, bear-elephant w/clever speech. "...born 'difficult' by temperament: highly sensitive, poorly adaptable, negative in mood, or disorganized." My feet have cracked like his.

1.17.92
DATE

44

Her

Pack car, clean up house, Isabel to day care, coffee with Carol, drive to Crestone and make good time, see lots of deer, get stuck in snow, walk a bit, a red-haired angel from the ashram picks us up in her truck and delivers us safely.

Conflict on seeing Robert. He is both nice and sharp. I feel instant rage, cry, make up, make love—he is tumultuous for me these days.

Isabel: I'm afraid of the mountains.

Me: Why?

Isabel: Are they jealous? Like the ladies in Cinderella?

Me: I think they are big but nice.

Isabel: Are they tired?

Me: Very very tired.

1.17.92
DATE

Him

Isabel's playing with her toys—they tell each other what color they are, and eat lunch, which turns out to be the decorative log in our room. Their faces turn brown. I give her a pretend napkin snipped from an envelope. "The napkin doesn't work," she says.

One of the college kids, Tracy, says Isabel closed the door of the atrium and told her, "We need to be alone so we can talk." What did you talk about? "Flashlights. For twenty minutes."

1.18.92
DATE

Her

Up and down emotionally, but sleep in until 9:30 A.M.—unheard of!
Ordinary monastery day:
Write a chapter
Walk to gold mine in snow
Start review book, revise essay, etc.
Various chats with various people, visiting college students
Robert builds Isabel a charming house out of a cardboard box—door
with handle, windows.

1.18.92
DATE

Him

Wretched night for Isabel. I woke with her sobbing by the bed and, in a sleep-addled way, decided she was asking me to take off her pants so she could pee. She stopped me. Miriam intervened, I re-slept. I think she was telling me she'd had a bad dream.

Shikunichi. Have Isabel from noon to closing today. We decorated the house I built for her, at her direction: she wanted a door and a window. I wrote "Isabel's House" and "Door," and she wrote a long story in glyphs and lines and scribble, about her friends and going to Santa Fe. We walked outside a bit. Roshi and Ulrike came by. He'd wet his pants falling in a stream while cross-country skiing. He kissed Isabel on her nose and me with his nose.

Lengthy discussion after our off-day breakfast about seminars, teaching and learning, and the too-masculine tone of things.

1.19.92
DATE

Her

Dream: about Woody Guthrie. A nice feeling. A man says, "We've burned the rivers halfway to Ohio."

Dream: I am looking for the four semiprecious stones prohibited in the Bible. Find them on a hill, shaped into tiny animals, fetishes, objects. Malachite and chalcedony are two.

The account of the dream is not the dream, the memory of the dream isn't either, even the dream isn't the meaning of the dream, and there is some kind of secret dream within the dream. But all of these things are the dream too, trying to surface.

Three years ago today I was in the hospital. My waters had broken, but I had not yet gone into labor. What does it mean, to say "I." The "I" of narrative. I've said it so many times, and still it remains slippery, transparent.

I'll write about what interests me, and not the truth.

Sat zazen last night happily for thirty minutes. Not much happened, and that's good.

1.19.92
DATE

Him

Last night we saw *Cyrano* with Gerard Depardieu and a lot of popcorn. Isabel and I said good-night to everyone and everything and slept well (lower temperature and better air circulation).

Packaged a black-ware pot with wooden crossbar that Lynne made for my mom.

Isabel told me while we were out walking, "When I was born the window was open and it snowed on my head and I cried and cried and Mom brushed the snow off my head."

Party with balloons and cake. Lynne outside our window with sparklers. Isabel happily blowing her party blowers and Steve jumping in mock alarm. The balloons were hard to inflate—is it the altitude? Air requires more compression and the strength of the rubber remains the same? It was good for the adults—loosened them up.

1.20.92
DATE I can't figure why people believe a bad time is more real than a good time, why one world is more real than another, or why Zen students who ostensibly accept the interpenetration of all things are obsessed with purity.

Reading from *Winnie-the-Pooh.*

Her

Last night saw the new movie of Cyrano de Bergerac, which made me cry, despite having seen it many times before and its inherent sentimentality.

Ruth, the German guest student, crashes right into me, no apology—this is the third time she has hit me or knocked something of mine over. A monastery is full of rudeness and grudges.

Isabel's birthday! She loves the baby dolls (tiny one from me, embroidered rag doll from Carol), the prince who matches Cinderella (i.e., Barbie and Ken dolls), clock, cassette player and tapes. All of these things go together as she plays. Lotto and alphabet book to be explored later.

Animal tracks. Weird dreams. That dream where I haven't been married, I've been single all these years...panic. I have to start dating.

Minor yeast infection.

Dreamed X. was dead and Y.'s mother said she didn't have to pay to go to the funeral.

Write chapter, book review, walk to gold mine, read Kath's manuscript on China, etc.

1.20.92
DATE

Him

Koan seminar at Steve's. Randy says, "When Roshi mentioned Bankei," and gives a long biographical speech—I mention Bankei, and interrupt with a question for Steve.

More presents today for Isabel—things I ordered arrived from Animal Town: animal stamps, animal masks. Steve gave her a small stone bear that belonged to Issan. Miriam was jealous.

1.21.92
DATE

Her

Moffat, Colorado, sits at the end of a narrowing valley, but still on the plain. The mountains to the east rise up so suddenly, huge and snowcapped, as if more than three-dimensional, but also moving in time.

Z. is thin and dark; when she reaches up to the top shelf her back arches like a dancer's. She has three daughters and has been married to both of the fathers. Her ex-husband is still in Brazil, an engineer. He builds roads. She cannot cook. She is middle class, and always had two maids. She wears a purple velveteen floral jacket, a bright flowered skirt, red socks. She drives a Toyota truck. She is leaving her second husband, the Moffat dentist, father of the third child, little Kim with the runny nose. The two older girls are M., a Cancer, and N., a Sagittarius. N. is too lively. Z. has long black hair. She separates daughters from fathers. I tell her: you look like a bird, a bright bird who has somehow flown into the snow. Z. is a Scorpio. She sends M. to the store, counting out change from a plastic baggie. She serves an odd treat of yogi tea, burnt cheese sandwiches, a chocolate over jelly cookie, and graham crackers. The little girls say they are hungry every five minutes. Isabel says the plastic soldier is her boyfriend and we all laugh uproariously.

1.21.92
DATE

The house is stucco, two large bare rooms downstairs, three small bedrooms upstairs. M. is the only one who sleeps alone. The house is for sale, it sits on the edge of the highway that runs north to Denver. Brazilian music floods the air.

Z: How do you practice Zen with children?

Me: I don't know.

Z: I am a mother. I am a mother.

Him

Isabel: "What's that on my pants?"
Me: "I don't know, maybe food."
"Maybe BOTTLE!"
"You're silly."
"YOU'RE plunky."
"What does 'plunky' mean?"
"Plunky means TICKLE YOU! Ha ha ha ha!"

Isabel steps delicately over the meal board on her way off the meditation platform.

Instant anger when Isabel falls and hurts herself. I know she knows what I'm feeling. Aaargh.

Dream: cutting up Charles Olson, who's shaped like a sausage, for dinner at Roshi's direction. The operative word was "proprioception."

1.22.92
DATE

Her

Hassle over February sesshin; Randy and Don want me out. Randy says: we don't want you to feel constrained. "We feel that way normally," I snap. Robert thinks I shouldn't use my psychic/social powers to judge what people are about to do; it isn't fair. That may be Zen, but it isn't me. I can read loud disapproval from many people here for me and Isabel, and I don't intend to ignore potential attack. Fuck them.

1.22.92
DATE

Him

Had Isabel much of the day. I spent the morning preparing baked apples for dinner while Isabel held court with the students sewing Roshi's robes in the greenhouse and sunning outside.

Laid out dinner during Roshi's afternoon seminar while Isabel grew more and more restless, finally flooding both counters then falling backward into the sink and banging her head. I was enraged, and threw a towel at her (at the counter next to her). Took her outside.

Miriam came in while I was setting out dinner for twenty and began asking me questions, letting Isabel run wild, asking me to serve her, and acting hurt when I refused and tried to set some limits.

Between dinner and zazen I read *Sipapu*. Isabel repeatedly came over and hit me, finally banging a book down on my shins. I picked her up and shook her and put her in bed—she was still sobbing when I left for zazen—Miriam said, "Would you like to make up with Dad," as the han was sounding and I was hurriedly putting on my robes.

1.23.92
DATE

Her

Dream that I am fucking X. and that Y. flies through the air. She is jealous and can no longer be my student. X. is a Zen monk, Y. is a writer. Wake up and just realize I am happy I was fucking this tall skinny solid man who is not, in reality, my type. Debora would say this is an animus dream.

Isabel with chocolate on her face.

Cat tracks, rabbit turds in snow.

Warm day.

Teach writing class—college students visit.

I'm not always aware that we're surrounded by mountains.

Often I just want to be left alone.

In writing class, Angelique writes a letter to a dead person—Dear Issan, you asshole. Dead, Issan is as wonderful as he was alive, and as much trouble—drag queen, Zen master, drunk, addict, saint.

1.23.92
DATE

Koan seminar—Roshi—case #17—Book of Serenity:

"I tell the students to divide their bodies in two, and look."

Him

Isabel was a little withdrawn this morning, attached to her mom as they prepared to leave. Cajoled her into affectionate behavior. They came in to say good-bye while I showered before breakfast. Isabel: "I can't hug you because I'll get WET so I'll kiss you good-bye."

Miriam calls at 2 P.M.—Isabel asks, "Are you still taking a shower?"

Shikunichi. Listen to tapes, write some letters.

Saw *Robin Hood.*

Had some beer with Angel in my room afterward and talked about being students, working with Roshi. Angel says he's terrified of intimacy. She advised me to practice being nonjudgmental about our compadres. Angel says Steve's nerves are shattered because he talked with Roshi for four hours about what goes on in the community—Roshi says it's all HIS problem.

1.24.92
DATE

Her

Drive home. Lunch in Tres Piedras in the white café. Santa Fe looks dusty, small, faraway, Spanish town. Exhausted and crabby. The house is fine and tidy but feels dead. Lilies of the valley bloom in a pot and smell sweet.

1.24.92
DATE

Him

When Mark raises the clappers at breakfast to start the meal chant, Lynne jams her hands over her ears.

There are fourteen people here. There were seven at breakfast this morning. We talked about Isabel. Mark asked me what I let her watch, saying he'd noticed we didn't shield her from violence.

Mark: "I wish Steve and Angelique would tell us when they're coming."

Randy: "Well, they're kind of silly sometimes."

Slept in the afternoon while the staff had their meeting. Read the *Wen Fu*. Called to Roshi through Ulrike's door after evening zazen, "When can I come by?" "Tomorrow?" "I'll come by tomorrow."

1.25.92
DATE

Her

Busy day. Isabel to Reuben's, teach first and second graders at Folk Art Museum, pick Isabel up, Renée comes to baby-sit, teach third and fourth grades until 4 P.M. Come home, collapse. Isabel goes to sleep at 5 P.M. and sleeps for fourteen hours, waking briefly twice. Robert calls. Feel overwhelmed. He says he loves me many times, but I feel all he wants from me is errands. It's confusing when I don't understand how I feel about him, angry but in a cool way, do I love him, what is a husband, what if I don't really need him, I've rearranged my whole life once again to suit him, etc. Debora Bluestone just says I want to get my own way all the time, probably true.

1.25.92
DATE

Him

Gossip has Roshi suggesting I be his *anja* (assistant). Steve told Angel told me. Angel and I discuss the ramifications while I'm making morning coffee. When breakfast is ready, I bring it up to him. "So," he says, "you think it's a good idea?" Yes, but I have to figure out about Isabel. "Angelique never worked more than half-time," he says.

After lunch, in the "break," I turn on the generator and go up to Roshi's room to xerox. He says, "One of the reasons I thought of you for this is that I won't be having the teaching seminar—too much community politics." I tell him I'd like to have the seminar. "When there's community politics, I'm gone," he says, leaving to ski with Ulrike.

Spent much of the day tracking down for Roshi a lecture published "soon after I came back from Japan," i.e., late '60s, in *Wind Bell,* filed in a box no one knows where. There are boxes in the shed, in the woodshop, all misnumbered. Tomorrow I'll call the *Wind Bell* office at San Francisco Zen Center.

Her

Tea at the Lambs'—Elizabeth looks well, Bruce peaky but better. He is eighty, and gives the impression that if he can live until spring he'll go another year.

Debora comes over, bearing playdough and needing coffee. Off to Children's Museum with Isabel. To K-Mart to buy underpants: nine pairs decorated with Little Mermaids for Isabel and seven pairs for me— pastel and floral.

Thaw yesterday, freeze again today. I feel tired again, chronic this time in town.

Cleaned out Isabel's dresser last night; amazing how she has grown. Clean bathroom, kitchen, bedroom; desk work for about forty-seven stolen minutes.

1.26.92
DATE

Him

Dokusan.

Cleaned out my room after work meeting, then went up to Roshi's. He says the job of the anja is to occupy the abbot's room, the way the *ino* occupies the zendo. I could sit in the room and do nothing except, "that doesn't work for Ulrike," so I should come up right after work meeting and ask if he needs anything. Did lots of cleaning: the slate around the fireplace with a damp cloth, the xerox machine, removed dead flowers.

Read Miriam's novel in manuscript last night. Has a good solid feeling, warm true detail. Up too late with it; tired today.

Long talk with Tom on the phone; asked him to sit Isabel while Miriam goes to her board meeting. I'm exhausted. Zipped up to Roshi's room to clean shelves with a dust cloth in the late afternoon. Many small things to remove and replace exactly.

1.27.92
DATE

Petra burned dinner soup (leftovers) by trying to heat it in a steam table pot. My head was swimming.

Gave up my room to the couple who run Haus der Stille and took last year's digs in the studio, which is another half step toward being fixed up: some couches, a few table lamps, less of a warehouse look.

Saw the mysterious thing they were trying to photograph yesterday: a $25,000 check from Q. in the lap of a Buddha figure. Q.'s getting old, says Steve, he's now eighty-two and trying to consolidate his involvements. How does he want to be involved with us, I want to know, worried that he too will decide to retire here. Financially, says Steve. Close to half a million dollars, but, considering who's involved, is that enough?

Her

Fights with various editors. Teach two lessons, errand for Robert at the college, take Isabel to look at sculpture in the mud, deep thaw, Miriam Bobkoff for dinner, tired but all right, too many fights.

1.27.92
DATE

Him

Less fatigued this morning, though I snoozed through zazen, as I did last night. Elaborate dream about huge Sagan house with round balconied platform hung over huge open stairwell. Luminous landscapes. Angrily yelling at Miriam in afternoon dream because Roshi had some odd, careful arrangement of open windows, placing himself so as to stay out of the draft; something blew out the door which she didn't retrieve. "Well I'm not a student," she sobbed.

"Individualism and miscommunication are deeply bound to one another." Ueno Chizuko, "The Technology of Love," *Kyoto Review.*

1.28.92
DATE

Her

Sleep happily until 8:15 A.M.
Isabel to day care
Teach edit femmes
Lunch at Cloud Cliff with Hope and Reuben.
I say:
>   What it means to be a woman
>   Without a husband—
>   Ice won't melt 'til spring.
Hope says:
>   That's a poem.
She looks gorgeous in red, with red heart earrings.

Tom comes to baby-sit. Go to the board meeting of St. Elizabeth's Shelter. Happy to be there. Isabel watches the "new" *Peter Pan,* the one with Mary Martin, twice.

1.28.92
DATE

67

Him

Day off, but I spent a lot of it in Roshi's room, xeroxing and arranging flowers, happily clipping back azaleas. He wants feedback on the book chapters right now—they're not too good, too rationalized a tone, none of the vividness of his lectures, the illumination of subtle practice and states of mind, "as if Buddhism were his dollhouse," Miriam once said.

Roshi told me that it was a fault of the pot that its lid broke when dropped. That the Hamada vase was worth two automobiles and the Japanese would carry it crouching over tatami so it would last the centuries. I thought of the vase as a swamp, and arranged very miscellaneous flowers: daisies, a spider mum, lily, carnation, tight yellow mums, in a reedy rising up out of the water.

"A taste is a promise," Roshi writes. Little tastes of landscape rising in my memory, each a place I've been, each with a feeling-tone, many in San Francisco. All the back of my head is full of places.

1.29.92
DATE

Spent two hours in the bathtub, drinking coffee, soaking, tired, then quickly shave my head. What are these major questions of Buddhism? What does Roshi mean by "inside and outside"?

Angel of Death's so close overhead I'm
    catching cold from the beating of his wings
When Buddha comes, I'll welcome him,
    when the Devil comes, I'll welcome him
But don't tell me Death's got no sting
    don't tell me what Death brings
Issan said, when you're dead you're
    dead, and there's no-thing.

My love is a bag of skin
Born to sickness, old age
    and death.

Her

Dream that I have a penis, large and white, it feels good and oozes a little at the tip. It only comes out of my vagina when I'm sexually aroused. My only problem: I can't for the life of me remember if this is normal, and if other women have them.

Buy one pair black sandals and one pair pink for the monastery.

Buy one lamp made out of a colorful basket for Isabel's room.

Thaw. Lovely melting weather.

1.29.92
DATE

Monica for dinner. She recounts a scary nightmare. Isabel says, shocked, "But where were your angels?"

Monica: "I don't know."

Isabel: "Don't worry. They are on your pillow at home."

Him

Went up to Roshi's room after service and talked for thirty minutes or so about his book. I always make the same decision: to say what I think, but to try to make it sound judicious. Roshi asks, but has trouble hearing it. When I came back with breakfast he taxed me for something I'd just said in the kitchen. It felt like a comeback for my criticism of his book. How does this stuff get back to him so fast?

1.30.92
DATE

Her

Sharon assigns me a story for the *Santa Fe Reporter:* "What Is Mental Health?" Fun to dig up quotes. Thoreau says: measure your health by your sympathy with morning and spring.

I always feel good in the morning, but afternoon is my low time, the time of day I was born.

1.30.92
DATE

Him

First day on more rigorous schedule: three periods zazen, *oryoki* (nested eating bowls) breakfast. I like the more formal, three-bowl ritual meal. Transferring it off the cushion, out of the zendo, and onto tables, with pieces of ceremony and an injunction to keep quiet, made me nervous, as if we should be doing something else.

Roshi gave me many slips of paper with incomprehensible book titles on them. I made a list and asked for clarifications. He was dismissive, finally saying he didn't want it now; maybe months from now.

Went to town to pick up his laser printer. Snow was blindingly bright. Played the *'59 Evergreen Review* tape in the Isuzu:

James Broughton—ex-Catholic

Rexroth—buzz saw voice, sentimental lefty/sexual pomes

Brother Antoninus

1.31.92
DATE

Philip sounding deep voiced, like somebody else, but the intonation is recognizable

McClure sounding callow

Ginsberg, a raving genius

Her

Wearing yellow stockings like a D. H. Lawrence heroine...

Ruts of dry mud, snow on the blue mountain, my tender black corduroy shoes.

I love my clothes.

This week fast and hectic, accomplished a lot—two kid workshops, two classes, three private lessons—but never quite experienced it all. A sense of forward motion without contemplation; no inner life except dreams and thaw.

Dream about old boyfriend Curtis. He turned away in his bed and wouldn't talk to me.

Isabel creeps into my bed the past few nights around 3 A.M. I don't have the heart not to let her stay, and she then sleeps well. She seems a little regressed—whiny, no potty. Is this commuting too tough on her? As a mother I still have to learn to trust: she'll grow. Also resist all that internal pressure, my father, scorn dripping from his lips, saying the word "regressed." As if our being babies and small children actually terrified him in some way, our helplessness.

1.31.92
DATE

It's wonderful to sit in the car and write, waiting for Carol at Cloud Cliff. A café is a wonderful thing, too.

Also—the color yellow	Isabel's cheeks
postage stamps	laundry lines
a map of London	full tank of gas
the public library	coffee

Off to the monastery this afternoon with Kath in caravan. At least all this coming and going sets weekly deadlines to clean things up and get things done.

Him

Violently ill last night. Ran out of the zendo and lay down, chilled and sweating. Had all my clothes on until ten, when I got up and puked. Sex an hour later with Miriam, at the end of which Isabel awoke.

Skipped morning zazen—weak, sweaty vertigo. "What'd I do yesterday," I ask Miriam, writing this. "Not much."

Her

Wild night. Robert is sick, vomiting. He feels better. We fuck madly. Isabel wakes up; she sobs and sobs. Midnight. I take her into the kitchen to talk. "Mama I *love* you, why won't you sleep with *me?*" Does she pick up the sex vibe? I feel we should be more discreet. Robert doesn't care. He thinks Isabel feels abandoned. She and I are cozy at home; she can come into my bed anytime; now I'm Daddy's. I tell her: I love you, I care how you feel, if I hurt you or made a mistake it's not because I don't love you. I say: I can't sleep with you, but here is a little piece of my heart for your heart. She sleeps for eight hours.

Should she be in the room with us? There is no practical solution. I'm worried about her; she seems five percent off, all this disruption. I do my best. Am I creating some suffering or drama for later? At home she is just stubborn. Here she has these big night terrors, is afraid of the picture on the wall, etc. I'm not sure what to do.

It's a pleasure to have Kath here for the weekend. She is a kind, serene presence with a braid.

2.1.92
DATE

Him

Still have the shits, sort of Day-Glo yellow. Enervated, but able to do the schedule except for breakfast.

Moved Isabel's bed next to ours, a better system than bumping her out of Miriam's bed whenever we're all together. Had Kath take her for an hour midday while we had a quick schtup.

Took Isabel around this morning on her wagon—came back from the shed with a load of small cardboard boxes for Roshi. We lay down in the afternoon while Miriam was teaching. I put on my glasses 'cause I heard her choking; she vomited all over herself, me, the bed, then wondered what was happening: "What is it? Spaghetti!" I tried to change the sheets and our clothes and manage her quietly; ripping an old pillowcase as I put it on the pillow, snarling at Isabel to shut up.

Talked to Philip briefly on the phone, which Roshi handed me.

2.2.92
DATE

Her

Write a chapter in a frustrated mood of interruptions.
Sex date with Robert while Kath baby-sits.
Give Isabel a bath.
Teach writing seminar.
Isabel throws up and has diarrhea, like Robert. Sleeps pink-cheeked.
Dinner. Read Marge Piercy and play polar bears in cave, baby dolls, etc., with Isabel, who has made a fast recovery.

Him

Entered the schedule at the wrong angle, somehow, and the rice soup was cold out of the serving pots and needed reheating. It got moved twice by other people; Ulrike filched the spoon off the tray in the hall; Miriam came in with Isabel ten minutes early and organized her breakfast looking harried. Why does my stomach always tense and I start to get angry when she looks pissy? I'll go back to posting signs and following the schedule completely, which has a real physical and mental groove. "Only dressing and eating should be points of more than casual mental application during the day," as the koan says.

Cup of hot milk for breakfast. Gerald teased me about it.

Trying morning with Isabel. Roshi came by and asked me to retrieve some lecture tapes containing a section on "the mood and muse of the day." Quickly. So I had to bludgeon Isabel, rather than waiting her out, as we went from one place to another; then keep her from wrecking Steve and Angel's small, luxuriously crowded den while Steve and I figured out where the riff might be. She fell several times, running up and down the hall, and finally jammed her toe in the swinging door. By the end of lunch I was ready for infanticide.

Miriam carries away Isabel, who's wailing, "No, no, put me down; I'm going to help Angelique ring the bell," while Miriam strides with her jaw set. I tell Isabel that she and I and Angel would ring the bell another time, okay? She considers this, stops crying momentarily, then reddens and sobs, "I want a BATH."

Roshi gave an incredible lecture about Vimalakirti's silence. I think he didn't prepare for it—he was at the post office, and the lecture was bumped half an hour, the house full of people with nowhere to go. I took

2.3.92
DATE

a shower. No intellectual pyrotechnics, just explication of the koan, about living in a nondual world, that roared with a sincere, impersonal power. Then ten minutes on Basho's "Frog jumps/water sound." I literally felt his words resonating in my gut. All about *approach,* about including yourself in the koan.

Isabel was asleep after *teisho* (lecture), and dinner was served ten minutes later, cleverly, all cold dishes. Miriam and I propped open the transom over the door, the hall door, and the kitchen door, a distance of about twelve feet, and went in to dinner. After dinner Miriam went and found the hall door shut and Isabel crying in bed.

> "You and me and Izzy
> and my mom-mie
> go to the mon-a-ste-ry
> go to my house
> you see, that's the story"
> —*Isabel*

2.3.92
DATE

Her

Wake up sleepy and overcast. But a good night—the second—big improvement ever since Robert moved Isabel's bed next to ours. A bit of snow. Type poems.

Write letters. Get mental health quotes for article. It's amazing how much can be done in an hour or two, though it sometimes takes a week to get that hour.

Take Angel and Isabel in to town for soda and candy treat. Angel depressed, all the games of dominance and control here. It's clear to me that the men really do boss the women around and that no one cares to talk about this. This little monastery often functions like a dysfunctional family. A sick version of playing dolls.

Stay up very late hanging out with Robert, Angel, Isabel, and the newly arrived Russell.

Him

Last night at dinner I said, "I'm good at many things, but making a living isn't one of them." Miriam said, "You married me."

Isabel and I played dolls while Miriam and Angel talked.

Russell arrived, looking handsome and tired.

Went out about ten, saw the hall lights toward the zendo, went to turn them off, and saw Roshi coming out of the zendo.

2.4.92
DATE

"Are you the night watch?"

"No," he said, "I always walk around at night."

I thought of how he'd said, "I never needed more than a few hours sleep." It's odd to think of him walking his domain at night.

Didn't hear any rolldown this morning—came charging into the zendo during the last rolldown with my mouth foul and nose full. One period and a funeral service for a relative of the woman who gave this property to the people who gave it to us.

At breakfast Mark and I were jiving around; called him "layman scum," which Isabel, to my surprise, repeated perfectly and meaningfully.

Shikunichi. We took the wagon out in the falling snow—Isabel in her red astronaut's jumpsuit and patchwork ski jacket and hood. Bright pink plastic boots. Red wagon. Gray world. Sleeping trees. We took the path the truck made to the septic tank below the garden.

Home Alone was the afternoon matinee. Isabel watched most of it, then played dolls off to the side, facing the TV. Russell and Mark saw the latter two-thirds. I wandered in and out, making sure Isabel was attended. Some of it worried her a little. Roshi came by for a minute, sat down, held her hand. Miriam saw the last fifteen minutes.

Found an old Hartford St. newsletter with a lecture of Issan's. Loving sad feeling to read and hear him talking about death, about knowing he was going to die, "I certainly am going to die," knowing he's dead.

A moth and two spiders. I removed one of the spiders into the hall.

Edward Scissorhands the evening movie. Miriam cleverly removed Isabel for the two to three minutes of major violence—I razzed her for it and she got mad. A satiric fairy tale with some real emotional content. Afterward chocolate cream pie of Dennis's.

2.4.92
DATE

Her

That dream again—the motel that sits out high in the middle of bare plains—always in the northeast corner of the dream. This time I'm running away from Joe-who-tried-to-kill-me in Boston. I go south for an hour; he follows me; I make a wild turn and go north again, lose him, end up in the motel trying to go in disguise. Pick up two long skinny cowboys in a pizza and beer joint, fuck them, suddenly a retarded girl appears. I try to get her to stop watching television and molest her by sticking a toothbrush up her ass. I decide I need to die/dye my hair.

Dream turns into a play; I am unprepared; my role is "second woman," barely a speaking part; I am scared and nervous. In the play the moon is made of cheese, and people make racist remarks.

Him

Mark had the boxes I'd been cutting down to size for video and computer disk containers for Roshi taken out and burned. I was enraged. I told him repeatedly that this was not all right, that it was hostile, that he was fucking with me, that we needed to talk about it. Angelique suddenly began shouting at him from the side that he couldn't treat me that way. I walked out of the room.

Gerald unclogs the drain into the septic line for the third time in as many days, snarling, "They're using toilet paper again." It's toilet paper they're pulling out of the elbow joint that gets clogged, and there's been a campaign to use less, if any at all. When Miriam begins to voice suggestions, he lectures her loudly and she bursts into tears. Isabel was worried; Gerald was contrite. Miriam refused to be comforted.

Lay ordination for Ulrike, Petra, and Ruth in the evening. All day long, the hostility in the air was thick enough to touch. I was folding lineage papers and the *sumi-e* covers for them when I heard Roshi upstairs yelling at Ulrike.

Miriam and I also fought, and made up. She was in bad shape. I suggested that the three of us go out for lunch, and she burst into tears. We went into Crestone. The car was stuck briefly on the road in the snow. New café's first day of business. We had a nice conversation: community problems, our feelings, plans, Isabel's schooling (Montessori or Shul preschool—I'd like her to grow up among Jewish people for tribal

2.5.92
DATE

80

identity), maybe going to Plum Village in France in a few years to practice in a Buddhist environment that explicitly includes children. "Besides," says Miriam, "we'll be in France." Working out a plan to do something about Philip's literary estate, despite that he won't make a will and doesn't care much about his oeuvre.

Mark apologized. We hugged. My eyes filled.

Angel told me Mir'd been sobbing in her room during the afternoon.

Was exhausted during the ceremony—felt benevolent, my eyes kept closing.

Afterward there was cider, fruitcake, a thick soy cream, and next to no conversation. My last pair of clean underwear was falling down so I changed out of my robes, put on a pair of pants, and wore a lone bright green undershirt in a sea of black robes, except for Roshi in his white kimono.

2.5.92
DATE

Her

Wake up well rested and fine at 9:15 A.M. Snow, about an inch, coating everything. Immediately stumble into problems. Have a fight with Gerald in the kitchen. The cess-line is clogged again, shit comes up in the greenhouse. I suggest this or that, but Gerald is convinced it is our communal fault, we flush toilet paper. So, he shovels shit. I suggest raising the water level. He yells. I cry. We make up, but too fast; I'm in a state. Robert fights with Mark, who has thrown his project of boxes out into the snow. Angel fights with Mark, etc., etc. Gerald hugs me; we apologize some more. I hate it here and want to go home. Robert and I almost fight. He suggests we go out to lunch, which is brilliant; we get stuck in the snow, make it out, go to the Road Kill Café, which has just opened in Crestone, and eat broccoli soup, roast beef, ice cream, coffee. Come back. Steve hugs me. Still hate it here. PMS. Verge of tears.

2.5.92
DATE

Petra and Gisela think I am right about the plumbing, want me to go to the staff meeting. Robert says the whole thing was not my business. So let them all get hepatitis. Keep Isabel out of there. Overcast. Evergreens. Snow, nothing moves. Lynne makes Isabel finger puppets. Mark acts friendly to Robert. I hate this world of unsaid tension. I can't be around it and not react. Lay ordination this evening—the group has wedding nerves.

Robert seems a paragon. Have I said I like him? He is thinner, handsome, and not bad with a stuck car. He seems more mature, somehow, and more open—being here appears good for him if not for me. Maybe the effect of therapy too. He says we could go to Plum Village for a summer with Isabel when she is older! Extraordinary idea—a Buddhist practice place that likes children (unlike here). I'm a peasant at heart. I don't dislike Gerald, and have indeed always faintly liked him, but this…

Obviously can't work today. Laundry. Visit with Angel. She literally trembles with rage. I cry. Roshi yells at Ulrike. Walk in snow. The sun is a flat disk behind snow clouds. Archaic, bronze torque or unidentified circle out of a Viking ship burial. Other people and their idiot opinions have gotten in my way too long. I won't give up my grudge, or I'd be dead. Some startled birds.

2.5.92
DATE

Him

Today's muse was sour. I couldn't shake the tired, marginless annoyed feeling, and took a lot of it out on Isabel, glaring, yelling, tossing her angrily onto the bed. Miriam was in her anguish mode—she only has one, and when she feels she's on the skids she stays in the desperate, crumpled, teary disaster state. When she feels a little better she's mean.

We had a long talk while Isabel slept in the afternoon, after I'd stomped off to seminar, and while we were talking I felt the mood lift. Isabel and Miriam and I took the wagon and walked down the road at dusk. Came back to the spanakópita Dennis made for dinner.

Preparing for the next five-day sesshin (in which there'll be no writing). We'll study during it, with a daily seminar, study periods, and Steve's teisho. Not the usual sesshin fare.

2.6.92
DATE Roshi's plane leaves 6 A.M. tomorrow from Albuquerque. There's some kind of meeting afoot with the estranged Zen Center crew in San Francisco.

I heard that Steve laid down a big number at staff meeting: that they were in retreat from the world and it was a change-or-die situation.

Steve: "Don't buy into anything. Hold to the forms of health. Of healthy situations."

After Isabel is asleep I'll be going up to help the boss pack. If Miriam and I can find a minute in the night we'll sneak off across the hall to the shower room for a quick fuck. The posted sesshin schedule has me doing breakfast dishes, hot water for tea, tea service in the afternoon, and doan all day one day.

Her

Really a horrible and punky day. Get period. Weep all day. Cry to Ulrike, who is very nice: already offered cappuccino and use of her room. Richard Baker-roshi comes in as I sob out my woe. He is also very nice. Later they both say they feel close to me. Cry on the phone to Miriam Bobkoff. Found out that Petra, Ruth, Ulrike sat silently all day next to our noisy room and no one warned me. Enraged. I don't want to represent "real life." I want choices. Ulrike says I should come back, that X. and Y. stopped having a marriage when she left Tassajara monastery for good. Long talk with Robert. He says I'm improved as a person, less crazy than I used to be, but still fall into despair. Walk with him, Isabel, in red wagon under the fingernail new moon at dusk. Isabel topples into a snowdrift, but is good humored. Sit zazen. Lynne baby-sits. Sit in Ulrike's seat in the corner by the altar, long shadows.

2.6.92
DATE

Her

Sesshin begins.

Work an hour in Ulrike's room, which is lovely and peaceful. Fold her white underwear as a favor.

Leave monastery around 11:40 A.M. Lunch in Alamosa: a steak sandwich at the Sands, salad bar. Isabel behaves delightfully.

Stop, low on gas, in Ojo. Very old man says: "Ah...*linda,* we have much gas but no electricity until four." Then to Isabel, who opens her eyes from a nap: "You look like a movie star!" Drive slowly and fill up outside of Española.

House is fine. Amaryllis still isn't in bloom. Talk to Robert, Hope, Miriam Bobkoff, Debora, my father. Isabel covers the kitchen table with toys, watches *Winnie-the-Pooh* movie twice, and other *Winnie-the-Pooh* movie once. Sort mail. No real biz, except *Coastal Lives* nominated for NM Women's Press Award. Two hundred and fifty dollars from class action suit on stolen car warranty (from 1986!). Immediately spend half on clothes from catalog. Crestone doesn't look too bad from this distance. Ha. Warm here, and the ice is practically gone from the front yard. Joe left a guitar next to the bed. Robert says he won't write in his part of the journal during sesshin. It's a jolt of energy to be home.

2.7.92
DATE

Her

Go to the Indian Museum with Isabel, not much to see, but statues in mud and snow are a big hit. Isabel identifies a statue with bow and arrow as Fox Boy. Fenn Gallery, which is a riotous mishmash of good and bad, much cowboy art, a Fechin, a gorgeous Taos School painting of an apple tree with little girl looking out a window, $25,000. The sculpture garden is extensive, a big pond with ducks, even a white peacock. Isabel kisses a series of small coiffed Indian ladies in red stone.

Tea with Debora and Gabriel. Isabel is regressed, jealous, sucks pacifier. Pretty amazing!

Miriam Bobkoff brings by Chinese food and her usual self. Seems to be doing well in her new life of apartment instead of Zen temple. Don't I know it.

2.8.92
DATE

Her

Desk work, valentines. Told Isabel: if you poop in the potty, you can have a present; what do you want? She says: a bear. Then poops. "It doesn't hurt." Buy her a pink valentine bear at Osco, who holds a red satin heart. Get the "new" *Peter Pan* movie again. Laundry. W. tells me she has done a pelvic exam as part of her midwife assistant training but has not told her husband, who will think she is a lesbian.

2.9.92
DATE

Her

Teach at Rio Grande. Kids are bad and wild. Restless nap while Isabel watches movie. Saw *Postcards from the Edge* last night. Watch *The Doors* movie in fragments—boringly psychedelic, but makes me think about rock and roll, arty garage bands, their effect on me, addiction, getting fat. Carol Moldaw comes to dinner and brings large exquisite tulips, pale red and white. Isabel goes restlessly to sleep at 6 P.M. Snow, rain —it's definitely February.

2.10.92
DATE

Her

Rio Grande kids behave slightly better. They have been lectured. A spoiled, unattractive bunch.

Mist in the morning. Ice on the windshield.

Edit femmes have the winter blues. Try to perk them up.

Yesterday spent sixty-three dollars in an attack of shopping. Got angry about Crestone, and bought:

1. bright yellow heavy shirt
2. royal blue big tailored sweatshirt

I believe in grammar, but no one else seems to. That is, I believe that the way I speak is fine and correct, and can be imitated in writing.

2.11.92
DATE

Him

Sesshin ended last night. Horrific under and overtones. Tension around its "study" aspect, seminars and reading, and about Steve as teacher. His lectures were frighteningly on target: us, emotionally, as practice beings not entirely in accord with each other—particularly on the level of what it is we think we're doing. This was amplified by our texts: two of Dogen's meditation manuals, the eighth-century Chinese text they're based on, and an essay analyzing the differences. Why are people so adamant that analysis is no part of Buddhism?

Seminars:

Steve: "...pay so much attention to the forms that you don't see what's manipulating them."

"It's naive to initiate yourself into the process and not take on the practices that make it work."

2.12.92
DATE

On yoga: "Buddhist practice is to disappear into Emptiness—it's kind of hard to do it if you're in touch with your body in the way you suggest."

On koans: "Challenge each other to stay in the meeting." And "To cut off your thinking is not what 'non-thinking' means."

Teisho: "All beings will thank you...for leaving them alone."

Thought of you
today while I ate
your cool touch
your hand on a plate

90

Her

Teach last class at Rio Grande elementary—valentines—wear silver pin of a hand holding a pink heart. Take Isabel to mall after day care and have a lovely time: library, doing puzzles, ride carousel, eat pretzels, buy earrings and a guitar hair clip for her, story hour, come home.

Saw Kath's new place—three big rooms, shady, old Santa Fe feel. Her tiny collections of shells, photographs; never saw her spread out before—her own space—she feels expanded and feminine in it, her Italian looks and big ceramic bowl full of oranges and acorn squash. She looks like a short story in her own house. Miriam Bobkoff also suddenly inhabiting her own apartment, only hers one big room full of globes and radio and a shelf of library books. Two women, both living alone with maps on the wall, no Virgins of Guadalupe. Kath's house feels more exotic, a sort of root cellar feeling, but domestic. Miriam's has collections too, rocks, rocks, and more rocks, and probably should have a helium balloon. Miriam lives on the surface of her house; Kath tunnels in. Miriam has that funny buoyancy; she likes to act as if she has no subconscious mind, and it gives her an affinity for things that actually don't, like mountains.

2.12.92
DATE

Him

Sleepy sitting during first period. Went into my room during kinhin and ate a candy bar Angel had left by the door. Drank a cup of coffee, slowly, sitting comfortably in the rocking chair in my robes. Buzzed through the remaining two periods.

Annoying work meeting. Angel was seething next to me as they dithered their way toward canceling afternoon study in favor of work because someone would have to fill the cistern.

Worked in the morning arranging office supplies for Roshi. Cleaned off some stacked open shelves and sorted stationery on them. Ate lunch as a mid-morning snack.

We rediscussed the afternoon schedule, decided to evaluate the way decisions are made. By work period it was snowing and windy—I napped all afternoon.

2.13.92
DATE

Turned out at dinner that no one had filled the cistern.

Randy says that the ino work here isn't much except during sesshin: to be in the zendo, aware of what's going on and who's in it, schedule the rotation of doans, make sure the altar is aligned precisely, "to give a feeling, when you offer the incense, of power and concentration; lining up Manjusri's nose with the nose of the Manjusri on the *thangka,* with Buddha's nose, with the incense in the pot, with the bowing mat."

Her

Morning off. Photocopy NEA grant, get my hair washed, cut, and sheen baked in. Rest in afternoon, teach at night. All this and single motherhood, too. Cold rain. The amaryllis cracks a red streak, but we leave tomorrow. I count the exquisite red and white tulips on the mantle and realize Carol's many small generosities to me. I've always been one to total up my friends, my best friends, like money or fabulous necklaces. A nice lunch with Joan Logghe, who took me and Isabel to Beckers. Isabel behaved. Joan was wearing a pink rose quartz necklace. Women fascinate me endlessly—their variety, their ability to cope.

Isabel: Am I a monk?

Me: You're a kid.

I: Daddy is a monk.

M: Yes.

I: And Daddy says Angelique is a monk *(said incredulously)*.

M: Yes.

I: And Steve is a monk.

M: Yes.

I: Why is Daddy a monk?

M: It's unusual, but it's his job.

I: Are you a monk?

M: No.

I: Why not?

M: My job is to be a poet, write, and teach.

I: Your job is to be my mama.

2.13.92
DATE

Him

Shikunichi.

Valentine's Day.

Petra left a cake, and called from Germany.

Steve says that Roshi has "a Dogen complex," and I laugh, under-standing: that urge to establish every detail himself, inability to delegate any small thing, absolute certainty that his preferences are RIGHT. Steve adds: "My teacher, the ancient Buddha, who died two years ago and you can't check anything."

Into town with Russell to mail books to Japan for Roshi, lunch at the Road Kill Café, where the bearded proprietor delivers a sermon on how the debasing of the currency is the cause of all evil and moral vagueness. He had us pegged as Crestone spirituals of some sort. I've heard that sermon from my father and was paralyzed, thinking only: hope this doesn't go on too long. It seemed unlikely (and paranoid).

Bath in the afternoon. Miriam and Isabel arrived early. Small squab-bles with Mir—she pushes and pulls around coming and going; wants to negotiate arrangements, prove our love, and settle in simultaneously.

Bounced checks in the mail from Santa Fe leave me queasy and feeling hopeless—can't figure out how it happened.

2.14.92
DATE

Her

Back to Crestone.
Punky feeling of reentry into the place.

2.14.92
DATE

Him

Quick vacuuming in Roshi's room for soji. Sesshin-style oryoki breakfast in the zendo. Spent study in the office, desperately telephoning—it's Saturday in the outside world, the bank is closed, but Miriam Bobkoff was home and agreed to deposit two hundred dollars Monday morning. I'll have to borrow it from someone else to pay her back. I have a list. Yike.

Morning with Isabel. Working out an agenda I've had—to suggest things to her, but let her roam free and follow her own head as much as possible. We played in the woods, visiting buildings with the wagon. The door of Don's one-room cabin seemed locked, so we peered in through the window and discussed what we saw: lots of Buddhist iconography in a room as small and orderly as a ship's cabin. Bed, books, desk dovetailed into each other.

2.15.92
DATE
We abandoned the wagon and took the less-traveled path back up into the mountain. Isabel asked me to carry her, said, "I'm going to be a BIG LADY, and Mom will get smaller and smaller and she'll be Isabel." We went to Joan's yurt on a shelf overlooking the valley far below. Inside, a low, spacious room with a mattress centered on a carpet on a bright finished wood floor. "A nice house," said Isabel. Took off our shoes and jackets and shared a chocolate valentine on the bed. Back toward the main house we stopped at the tractor to pretend driving it into the far mountains and up into the treetops. "It can go up in trees if they're not too big," said Isabel.

Wade through snow in the garden carrying Isabel to the teepee. We crouched inside for a long time. Isabel brushed her teeth, pulling the supplies out of her handbag, along with two hair bands, which she asked

96

me to bunch her hair with, "like Pippi." There was a papier-mâché mask hung from a pole, which I explained was to keep the house company. The walls were mildewing, holes rotted open.

We went back for the wagon in the trees and trekked around to the dome, its big bentwood arch all roof and skylight. Inside we were birds on the canvas floor, holding our arms out, running, yelling "FLY! FLY!"

Early afternoon Russell took Isabel, and Miriam and I went off to the yurt for brief practiced parental sex.

Her

Walk to the yurt that Joan Halifax built, Robert carries a quilt in a duffel bag, take off our clothes in the cold and fuck ourselves silly, mind-popping, look up and see a hole in the sky, going fuck me fuck me on my back.

2.15.92
DATE

Andrew Franck wrote Robert a letter saying he'd had a dream about wearing a red shirt and about a cutthroat trout. I think of the amaryllis's slash of red.

Him

Snowing today.

Isabel woke up looking grave and quiet, only asking if she could have some raisins for breakfast. She came back from her four-minute shower looking sad. I hugged her and rubbed her back for a long time. "What," I asked, "are you thinking?"

"I'm thinking about my house."

"After we leave the monastery we're all going home together."

"You too?"

"Yes."

"And Mom?"

"Yes."

"And me too?"

"Yup."

2.16.92
DATE
She brightened. "I wrote to my house yesterday."

"A valentine?"

"Yes! You want to see?"

Shower and work meeting. Gisela announced that Bonnie had returned from the hospital in Denver with her "female organs, I can't remember the word, taken out," explaining that her mother had taken drugs to have her and she knew she was at risk, though beyond the time it usually showed. Gisela said, "It's sad," and burst into tears. The meeting stood silent. I rubbed her shoulders for a while. I remember Bonnie from shopping in Alamosa for sesshin, pretty, longhaired, bruised looking. Miriam said, "DES; she's dead."

Two-hour afternoon all-residents meeting. The joint is out of money. Can't plan income or fund-raising without being able to tell what we are or what we're going to do. Also, Roshi's leery of outreach. Steve says, "Not knowing about the future, then you just extend the present." Lots of discussion of the schedule. Steve: "Once you have some feeling of the integrity of the schedule, then you can make changes. It's the baseline of our practice together. You make decisions about the schedule in relation to other people. You have this inner question, and if you discuss it, the inner question dissolves. It's not asking for permission."

The second half got bogged down in dog issues, i.e., how many dogs do we keep around the place, what kind of toilet paper shall we buy, trivia that can be discussed endlessly. We talked about washing dishes: air-dry or wipe, Clorox rinse or not, vinegar. The process drove me crazy, and the surfacing of the purity ethic, all fear of poisoning and half-understood notions, while the discussion was carried by those with the most conviction and endurance.

Isabel had a shower and two baths and several small tantrums in the late afternoon and early evening.

2.16.92
DATE

Her

Snow in the morning.

Community tension. Both Lynne and Gisela in tears.

Ulrike's room is a godsend. Saves my sanity. I can be alone. The yurt date was fun, too.

Dream I had passionate sex with X. and Y. refused to fuck a boy up the ass. (This had something to do with publishing.)

Talk with Steve, who feels we are caught up in other people's karma here, a series of trip lines.

Make snow ice cream with Isabel: snow and vanilla and half-and-half and sugar and maple syrup. Not bad.

Snow all day. A medium feeling of boredom.

2.16.92
DATE

Him

Dream I've taken up with Lizzie Gray—she's lying in bed—don't want her to take Isabel, who looks anxious, away by the hand.

Isabel: "Why is the door locked? So I don't escape?"

Her first shave—standing in front of the bathroom mirror, using my cream and bladeless razor handle.

Big simmering fight all day with Miriam—money, travel, taking care. Decided finally to abandon each other, get divorced. Cheered up. Made up.

Talked to Julie for an hour on the phone, borrowed two hundred fifty dollars.

Found .30-.30 shells in Roshi's bathroom closet when replacing the vacuum. Where there are shells there're often guns; I found the rifle in among the two-by-fours. Either it's a leftover from Lindisfarne, or it's Roshi's last line of defense.

2.17.92
DATE

Steve: "The important thing is to know when it's *not* in the closet."

I: "The important thing is to know where the bodies are buried."

Isabel kept announcing at dinner that her dad was mad at her mom.

Her

Robert wants to borrow money—two hundred dollars plus. I don't want to give it. It doesn't feel appropriate; he bounced the checks, never pays me back. Feels good to say no, but scary, too—will he punish me for this somehow? I feel sure Fred (our therapist) would support my not giving him the money. For January-February-March of this year—

I pay:
mortgage, all house bills
Isabel's day care
my fees here
gas
I lend Robert:
his fees here
his health insurance
This feels like enough.

Later—big fight ensues. Robert says he is not going to London with my family next summer. I say we are breaking up. He grabs me angrily. We make up.

I should have known—break unspoken contracts and the other person will try to make you suffer on some level. I'm sick of him.

Zazen.

Him

Sometimes I feel I'm practicing a different religion, or a deeply different Buddhism, from the long-term residents. They have such an emphasis on purity, rejection of the world and the senses. "They think Buddhism is a nondairy diet," Miriam says. I suggested to her that what we see in them as rigidity and hatefulness might just be the absence of any emphasis on Mahayana interpenetration and compassion. "It lacks rigor," she said, "and you're calling it wrong. It's Christianity. Platonic split, boychik."

Gerald is work leader—asks if I need extra help. I say, maybe later. When I ask for help he says, basically, do it yourself. Later I ask for Russell, and am assigned four people, two of whom never show and one who wanders away after fifteen minutes. Russell and I perform prodigies of cleaning on Roshi's very dusty room and get most of it done. I rub down half of the stairwell walls with baking soda.

2.18.92
DATE

Letter from Philip.

Foreclosure notice from the mortgage company for Dharma Sangha temple in Santa Fe.

Isabel gives Randy an abstract painting for his birthday. "What is it?" he asks. "Paint!" says Isabel.

Half hour with Isabel being polar bears in a blanket cave. When I offer to eat her, she says, "Are you hungry? Have some FISH! Delicious!" Her cannibal number is a little frightening in its intensity.

She's been asking, "Tell me the story of the little girl who is sick," the shaman curing scene from *Indian Tales,* over and over.

Isabel claimed that the corn bread I gave her for dinner *wasn't* corn bread.

Gerald: "It is corn bread; I cooked it this morning," in his hectoring voice.

"I'm not talking to you," staring him in the face, "I'm talking to my daddy."

"It is corn bread, I know, I'm the one who made it."

"I'm not talking to you, I'm talking to my daddy."

General laughter.

I suggest she tries it. She does, begins eating it.

To Gerald: "I know it's corn bread," putting the needle in.

2.18.92
DATE

Her

A definite feeling of boredom, what am I doing here, it doesn't make sense, etc. This kind of concentration is not my kind. The whole thing feels ludicrous. Writing novel revision goes hard, too.

Wake up with Isabel 8:30 A.M. Breakfast with serving crew in kitchen, hot cereal and tofu scramble. Isabel plays in atrium, all her plastic animals on the dry well around the big tree.

9:45–11:00 A.M. work in Ulrike's room. Notebooks, calendar, type a short chapter.

11:00–11:40 snack in kitchen. Angel and I bounce ball in atrium, old girl's song: "A my name is Anne, my husband's name is Andy, we come from Argentina, to bring you…APPLES!"

11:40–1:00 bath with Isabel. Visit Ulrike's room. Isabel builds "rocket ship" with tiny blocks. Cherry coke. White panty hose with black polka dots.

1:00–1:45 lunch, with chocolate cake for Randy's birthday.

2:00–2:30 read.

2:30–4:00 writing class.

Walk to gold mine.

Evening, stories, and bed.

2.18.92
DATE

Him

Shikunichi.

N. ran some number on Miriam this morning, refusing to turn on the generator for her to do her laundry. She was a wreck. I was phoning around about the mortgage, and foolishly attempted to comfort her in the midst of my own blind rage. Miriam Bobkoff arrived and took her off.

Isabel and I piled in the car and went to Salida—the north end of the valley rises and narrows, the snow-covered mountains are deeply beautiful, and I left my bad feelings behind. We drove up through Poncha Pass, down into Poncha Springs, and east to Salida—Isabel was asleep, so I bypassed the First St. Café (where, it turned out, the two Miriams had run into Steve and Angel and were having lunch). We drove around town for a while. My heart leapt, seeing a slightly decrepit small brick house set in the trees.

2.19.92
DATE

Driving through the pass, Isabel wanted to know, "Where are the polar bears here?"

Told Isabel that her mom and I loved her and were going to make sure she had a good life. She said, "In the car?" We talked about learning to drive—I promised she'd get a learner's permit when she was fifteen. "I can drive *this* car?"

Miriam and I had our halfway talk. Told her this was important and I'd rather stay, but we could go home if she had to, or work out some other arrangement. She's not in good shape—too much time in her panic state.

Long pleasantries in our room with Miriam Bobkoff, Miriam, Russell, and Isabel in the evening.

Her

Complete misery, breakdown, can't stand being here. Tears. N. won't let me do laundry. Miriam Bobkoff comes up and takes me to Salida. Feel Robert and I are getting divorced. Feel I am losing it, a bad mother. Buy Isabel two dinosaur pencils, dinosaur coloring book (tiny, with crayons), dinosaur pencil case, troll. Eat hamburger. The San Luis Valley narrows beautifully at the top as ranges of mountains come together, and beyond that much warmer, Arkansas River, red showing on the tips of trees, and no snow.

2.19.92
DATE

Him

Had Don speak to N.—he did well. Miriam did her laundry. Isabel has clean clothes again.

Went to Crestone with Isabel and procured Muppets movie. Car stuck and overheated on return.

Staff meeting in afternoon. I attended as ino, first day.

Many phone calls re: mortgage. UMCO called, are beginning foreclosure proceedings.

Her

Wake up tense.

Nice to have Miriam Bobkoff here, even briefly.

Handwash. Many discussions about laundry.

Write a floating chapter.

Visit with Angel in the afternoon. She paints my fingernails dark purple, and the fingers of Isabel's left hand.

Muppets movie.

Stay up late talking to Robert, Dharma Sangha mortgage crisis, etc., and fuck in an empty room.

Recorded my poetry in the dome, sounds good.

2.20.92
DATE

Him

Doshi (officiating priest) last night and this morning. Not too precise, but okay, coursing in feeling.

The mechanism that points the solar panels at the sun was tracking the moon all night.

Spoke with Roshi briefly on the phone this morning. He's holed up in the AMFAC Hotel in Albuquerque, writing his book. Doesn't want to be called unless it's an emergency—resistant to treating the mortgage as a crisis.

Went to town with Isabel, incidentally separating dogs Rufus and Janie and returning Rufus to Sally at the store. He leapt back in the car each time I opened the door.

Slept through lunch and into seminar. Angel and Russell asked me a lot of questions about the case, "Vimalakirti's Silence," in Steve's absence.

2.21.92
DATE

Housecalls in the Fragrant Land

Manjusri with his sword
Vimalakirti with his family
Hold open between them a gate of kindness
Manjusri stands in fields of color
Vimalakirti in darkness
Before a dark window
His silence—thunder
His wife named Golden Lady
His child, Moonlike Beauty

His intestines bleeding
Good days and bad days
What wisdom sees
Is suddenness, then nothing
For all beings, all people
Manjusri come to see the sick layman
Saying, "According to my mind, in all things"
Between them is death
Going down in darkness
Exhausted, not knowing
Touching death dark with their bodies
Bringing it up together

Her

2.21.92
DATE

A morning of phone calls. Not much desire to write. Have done six chapter drafts so far this stint.

Clear and bright. Antsy. Is the car all right? Robert overheated it and boiled off radiator fluid. Low on gas. He takes it into town to fill it up. I'll be glad to go home. But somehow it is also hard to extricate myself from sticky monastery.

Nice walk with Isabel. We find a large stalactite of ice formed by drips from the gutter on the wood shed. It has a hollow center. Isabel says it is a piggy bank, and then she gets stuck in the nearby mud, which pulls off her boots. I lift her out barefoot and laugh—New Mexico spring in miniature. Come home and take a long hot shower in Baker-roshi's tub, which is big and tiled. We enjoy ourselves.

Him

Irritable this morning.

I officiate at morning service.

Isabel's been listening over and over to the tape of her singing rhymes, lip-synching, repeating things off the tape, talking to herself: "Hello! That's my friend Isabel. That's me! And you and mom!"

We three went to Salida for lunch and to the dinosaur store. Isabel had a fit of the greedies: "Which one do you want?"

"I want many. Many many."

Miriam and I talked solidly for the hours there and back.

Isabel: "Daddy, I want to call you Robert."

ANGER:

I saw myself holding a plate and snarling, about to smash the plate, a shaven-headed priest, and thought, this looks ridiculous.

2.22.92 DATE

I see the consequences to Isabel along with the anger, and back off, over and over.

A lot of my anger here is triggered by objects.

There's some curious way the teaching inheres in objects and relationships. The style here is, if you want to fuck with someone, you do it with things, not ever directly.

The flowering of my anger's accompanied by the phrase "I've had enough," the feeling of being pushed beyond what it's reasonable to endure.

Long talk with Steve before evening zazen: how to do service—where to bow, when to walk in *shashu* (hands folded), what's up with Roshi, approaches to staff meeting.

Three people in zazen tonight. Some sick in bed: Angel, Gerald, Dennis; some at the talent show; Lynne, Gisela, Roshi, and Ulrike away.

Her

Don't write. Have done seven chapters this stay. Could the immersion in painful subject material account in part for my depression. All family members cranky. Decide we will go to Salida for lunch. Cheer up.

Robert read to me from his diary. Weird bits touch and cross. I suggested that today we both write about anger.

Anger. When I get really angry, I have to lie down.

Fred gave me the mantra: I have a right to be angry. I'm not even up to the rest: I have a right to express my anger *and* if I'm angry and express it I am not a bad person.

2.22.92
DATE

Things that make me angry at the monastery:
being cramped in one room
other people's bad vibes
limited access to laundry
being told what to do
Isabel in a bad mood, demanding
Robert ignoring me
no seasoning on the food

Things that generally make me angry:
racist remarks
social injustice

the post office
bad waiters
mean editors
Robert hurts my feelings
Isabel has a fit
rock and roll gigs
ecological disaster
trash on the beach
being stood up
other people being late
being late
Reform Judaism
cars break down
plumbing breaks down
rejection of my work

bad drivers
doctors
my classes resist me
people owe me money
something I like is torn or broken
other people are jealous of my success or child
anyone criticizes Isabel
food craziness
drug dealing
people who claim to be incest victims who aren't
being told I am fat
paying bills
bouncing checks

taxes
parking tickets
parties I have to go to
the past—Dwight School, childhood
anti-Semitism
being pulled over by a cop
old lovers
people who believe reincarnation explains oppression
New Age medical advice
being told I am a bad housekeeper

Things that almost never make me angry:
supermarkets and checkout ladies
Virgin of Guadalupe
books
flowers
earrings
shopping for clothes
carousels
the ocean
hot baths
hot springs
suspension bridges
other people's babies
sex
fruit juice
coffee
ferryboats

2.22.92
DATE

115

big storms
rain
getting mail
going for a walk
dancing to rock and roll
sleeping
ladies' lunch
trashy magazines
museums
drawing
writing
being outside with Isabel
being unrushed with Isabel
New Mexico
San Francisco

2.22.92
DATE

the idea of travel
Kath
Hope
Robert loves me
spring
my birthday
any sort of present
cheap shoes
pickles, kim chee, chiles, etc.
cats
birds, domestic and wild
mineral specimens
things that belonged to dead people

Does zazen dissipate anger?
No.
What am I afraid of?

Him

Roshi: "Entering by the gate of power
Leaving by the gate of kindness"

Miriam was harsh and expected me to be loving as she left with Isabel. Another squabble.

Morning work period getting ready for Roshi's return, now scheduled for Monday or Tuesday, "at the latest." Cleaned Ulrike's room after Miriam. Did the family laundry. Angel continues to put off showing me how to fold Roshi's robes. Began organizing Roshi chores—typed a long list from many slips of paper.

2.23.92
DATE

Staff meeting: how to take care of drop-in students and guests.

Lynne came back from ten days of working in Bertha's pottery studio looking totally blissed out. Gisela back from her lady friends in Santa Fe full of movie plots.

Finished cleaning Roshi's stairwell. Can't figure out when to fire up the stove—it takes about three hours to get that frozen room up to speed.

Light snow today.

Her

Split from Crestone. Easy enough drive. Feel spring in the Española valley, then it starts snowing as soon as we get home. The amaryllis is in dazzling bloom, five huge striped peppermint blossoms. I remember the amaryllis when I was a child, green shoot that just kept on growing. Rosie had to put the pot on the floor, it was too tall for the plant shelf. Was my mother gone? It was this time of year. Some feeling that she would be thrilled to see the flower, but didn't. Europe? Or gone to Boston that dreadful winter she left for two months. Perhaps no coincidence I now have an amaryllis she sent in a pot.

2.23.92
DATE

Shop. Fifty dollars on groceries. Cook chili. Isabel poops in the pot—second day in a row.

2.24.92
DATE

Him

Shikunichi.

After service I puttered in Roshi's room, cleaning around the stove, put on Robert Johnson tape and folded Roshi's gold silk robes on a sheet on his bed.

Drive to the pizza place in Salida with Russell: a two-story Georgian public building converted into a house. A living room full of Victorian furniture with a Formica pizzeria in back. The ultimate mom-and-pop store, as Russell said—mom and pop stood at our elbows through the meal.

Waiter at the First St. Café remembers how I like my coffee, but he's still vague about the menu. Find a Burton Watson *Han Shan* for Russell and a space opera about an interplanetary circuit court judge for myself in the used bookstore. We admire the brick buildings, buy flowers for Roshi's room.

Lynne's unfired pots spread out on the kitchen table. She says firing melts and fuses the glass in the clay. The blue clay we sent years ago from the Vineyard will be glaze, though it may not fire blue. "It depends on why it's blue. If it's blue from carbon it just burns away."

Gerald has spontaneously put me back on the soji list. I hate having to renegotiate everything all the time—I've been anja for a month, going up to Roshi's room every day instead of soji. Russell points out that the person listed to clean the atrium is the atrium.

Don says he wants to clear something up: Why am I coming to staff meeting? Who did I talk to about it?

I explain, calmly as I can, that for the next month I'm the ino, that I'd spoken to Randy as ino when he bade me go to the meetings as part of the job, to Steve about the meetings themselves; that there was some question about how much of a monastery this was, but in a Zen monastery the officers met as part of the schedule, and it was the office that was important, not the people.

2.24.92
DATE

He said, "Well, I guess we'll clear it up tomorrow."

Angel says she can't take any more of the endless harassment and hostility toward her as a woman and is leaving, but waiting to talk to Roshi. I wish she would stay, and offer my support, suggesting she go off the schedule. She says the schedule's not the problem, the people are.

Dream: cutting gray basalt with a chisel, smoothing down the sides— it was going to be a life-size sculpture of Suzuki-roshi, but I'm saying it's better like this—Lynne reassures me. (The koan says, "Polishing a tile to make a Buddha.")

Her

Some night terrors, both me and Isabel. I have a long dream about *Almanac of the Dead,* that extraordinary book, in which the dream itself has the title "Indian Dreams" and Russell is going out with Leslie Marmon Silko, who isn't very nice to him.

2.24.92
DATE Isabel to school. Mysterious snake cage appears on porch—returned by Kristina? Gas in car. Phone calls. Allen Ginsberg on tape. Wine and cheese with Kath, her mom and dad. I can feel how she has made herself up, as have we all, second-generation Americans.

Him

Meeting with Steve. We hear Angelique and Gerald have a long, screaming fight at the other end of the building. Angel comes in white-faced, eyes wide, nostrils flared. Steve is pale and shaking. I turn the heat way up.

2.25.92
DATE Miriam: "It's not hard to be a saint. All you have to do is be twenty percent more open, twenty percent more random and out of your personality, and you shine. Like Issan."

Angelique was the last item on the agenda at staff meeting. Steve said that she intended to leave. Lynne and Gisela made speeches about the energy of the mountain, and how women needed to adapt themselves to it. Lynne said her experience was that all her problems had been internal resistance to being told what to do in practice. Steve replied, "Don't put yourself down."

Gerald told us that we old-time students were trying to re-create the old Zen Center, and knew the old Baker-roshi, not the new one, and had come in making changes without pausing to see what was going on.

Steve said, finally, "I'm a Zen teacher. I'm not coming from the conventional. I didn't intend to be on the staff; Roshi asked me to be head of practice. And you never asked me anything, you never consulted with me, you were never friendly."

Gerald said, "No one pushes without someone pushing back."

I: "Gerald, it's not mechanical. It's not an equal and opposite reaction. You have a bullying manner. I've known you long enough to know that you're also kind, but you push more than you're pushed."

He was red-faced, eyes shiny, features pushed together toward the center of his face. Gisela was crying and angry, saying, "I'm a guest in this country, and Angelique says to me, 'Fuck you.'"

I said it's been very difficult to practice here, and the problems were primarily social; a lot of pushing and shoving across the varying arrangements of the schedule, etc., that Gerald was the conduit for a lot of the hostility coming out of the core group and aimed at it, both, because he was the worst example—but they all did it, all the time, and they'd driven many people away. Gisela said they never had; it was only Angel, me, and Steve who had a problem.

Don thanked me after, saying Gerald and Gisela had almost driven him away twice, and that he'd long since given up on practicing within a group.

Gerald got up during evening zazen and strode out, slamming doors so that the building shook. Gisela followed. A cluster of four or five people stopped in the kitchen on their way to bed after zazen, ten minutes later, and sighed once, all together.

2.25.92
DATE

Her

Edit femmes—such a great group. Very lively. They notice that my novel is full of people smashing glass. It is.

Y. complaining about the homeless on the streets in San Francisco. "We had to give up our opera subscription." Really. St. Elizabeth's Shelter meeting tonight.

Things I keep leaving out:

Joe says: the kid *is* the dharma.

The double-trunked tree, or two trees grown completely together, at the catty-corner neighbor's across the street.

A Buddhist fear: fear of finding yourself in a body.

Hypochondria: lumps, moles, waking up each morning surprised I am alive.

Shadow motif in fiction: how things imitate each other, as indeed they do, preposterously, in life.

2.26.92 DATE

St. Elizabeth's Shelter: take a tour, smells like linoleum and meat loaf, doughnuts and not washing. Board meeting: should St. E's continue to house "the mentally ill," i.e., crazy people who see Jesus on your left ear, not just your usual person crazy without a home.

Him

Gerald and Gisela came early to morning zazen.

Roshi arrived during the night, and I made him and Ulrike breakfast and brought it over. Russell and I went up during work period, each with our lists. I put "we're having a crisis" as the last item on the agenda, right after "who do we have sign checks on the Santa Fe account?" Told all, at length, with Russell there and Ulrike for part of it. He listened, said only two things: "Gerald's driven a lot of people away," and "I'm not very good at understanding or picking up people's emotions."

People were oddly kind for the rest of the day, Mark making a slice of bread and butter with jam and feeding it to me, Gerald going out of his way to be my *jisha* (ceremonial assistant), etc. Gave Gerald a hug in passing.

Steve took to his bed after breakfast. I went over with a snack and talked to them, nabbing a pocketful of pretzels. He looked and sounded genuinely awful, the psychosomatic part notwithstanding.

There was a seminar instead of the all-house meeting we'd planned. I was a little punchy.

Ulrike said that Roshi proudly showed her the bathrooms at Greens (which he designed). I said Issan'd shown me where to stand in the hall at Roshi's Desert Cafe to see men at the urinals.

Roshi and Ulrike bought all kinds of things at the Price Club in Albuquerque: a vacuum, cardboard file boxes, which I put together, an ironing board (Ulrike says it makes her feel empowered to have her own ironing board), and apple strudel, which we had for lunch.

Roshi is auditing Steve's sesshin lecture tapes—Gerald complained. Feel relieved, as if telling all the principals and Roshi let me shake my involvement—the upcoming thrashing out is just another knotty part of the schedule.

Her

Fine day at home—interview at Folk Art Museum, tea with Sabrina, Reuben for dinner, catch bad vibes from the monastery long distance— the shit hit the fan; Angel exploded at Gerald; the "in" crowd tells "our" crowd: "you represent the old Zen Center." Even at this distance I can't stand it. Robert sounds edgy, but seems to be holding his own nicely.

Him

Doshi again.

Five hours sleep, enough. Half of what sleep I normally get seems fine, though I'm drinking many cups of lapsang souchong, black currant, oolong tea, coffee, mixing lowfat milk with half-and-half. I can always tell when a European's made the coffee; it's an order of magnitude stronger, better that way, with the woody bite of the beans coming through the milk.

2.27.92
DATE

Angel says, "Steve would like to see Roshi," insisting I get to him RIGHT NOW. Roshi says, anytime. I tell Angel to send Steve up. Several hours later I ask Angel, "Is he still up there," and she says, "Did you talk to Roshi?" Much charging back and forth to patch things up, Roshi waiting, Steve slighted, Angel fried to a crisp. I'd spent the morning finding things to do outside Roshi's room.

Roshi is paying out $2,500 to have the rotting bathroom in the Santa Fe temple fixed—I ask him if he's sure he wants to do this while the foreclosure's going on; he says, "Oh, we'll keep the temple no matter what." Asks me to leave while he's talking on the phone because, "I feel I'm excluding you."

Miriam Bobkoff on the phone: "Don't underestimate how scared they are. If they're thinking of it as an *us and them* situation, if they lose they're out."

Her

Toward morning, tense dream about my old boyfriend Lewis, the monastery, Baker-roshi has shackled my hands together with a straw vise during zazen. I am very angry, and blame him in public.

Wake up 8:10 A.M. Isabel in school thirty-five minutes later! I have even taken out the garbage, but not eaten.

2.27.92
DATE

Him

Blam. Roshi was, in one swoop, highly critical of my anja-ing: "If you can't do it, maybe Angelique…" Ino-ing: "Sitting facing out is a much higher position than ino. It doesn't go with the job." My crisis management: "I've heard that you're the ringleader of the Santa Fe group, and that you said they have contempt for the people here," and my having gone into Ulrike's room to confer with Steve and Angel.

I explained what I saw, but felt that my take on the patterns and emotional life of this place had lost any credibility. I'd conferred with Randy and Gerald, both, about sitting facing out into the zendo; I'd quoted Miriam Bobkoff saying she felt the Crestones had contempt for us. He said finally that we had to create harmony to work from, and I should go now to work meeting. I left with my mouth open.

2.28.92
DATE

When I came back I asked him how to practice with this stuff—I'd heard him say, keep each thing separate. He said to concentrate on each object, for example a piece of paper handed to me, first, and the secondary subtexts second; to treat hostility very carefully, or it would cause a conflagration.

I'm very clearly out; the good tea bowls are now too valuable for me to carry downstairs and wash, and no, he doesn't need any help today. He added that I'm too Japanese in the zendo, too hard and inward, being centered was okay, but to try and include everyone else more.

"Favor and disfavor both belong to the land of dreams," says Muso Soseki.

Talked to Russell and Steve, who says his interview went well, but it's too soon to tell how things will fall out or if they'll just be swept under the carpet. He and Angel seem much improved.

126

Found a good box, or most of one, for Roshi's giant ceramic *kobaku* (incense pot).

Roshi called me into Ulrike's room to shout at me for letting Olaf clean his and her rooms, throwing away her dying poinsettia, cutting back his azalea. "She's upstairs, right now, sick. She's talking about going back to Germany. She says this is a madhouse."

Roshi: "My room upsets people...I feel violated. You don't seem to know without being told. You've been to Tassajara, you've been at Zen Center." I said I'd never practiced at Tassajara, and never seen an anja working close up, and apologized. He said shortly, "It's fine," and walked out. Told him also that Gerald had assigned me two helpers, but not that I'd consulted with Russell and Lynne about the plants. Miriam Bobkoff called, that experienced anja, and her verdict was, "a mistake, but not usually lethal."

Went up after lunch to give Roshi his mail and see if he needed anything—waved me away.

2.28.92
DATE

Steve said he'd described me to Roshi as Robespierre to Gerald's Danton. Thanks a whole lot.

Roshi listened to lectures #4 and #5 and criticized him for paraphrasing Dogen without attribution, for being too harsh toward the end, but said that he could hear his voice in Steve's.

Roshi gave a seminar on Vimalakirti that was about our troubles in a subterranean way. His instruction: do some small thing in each unit of the day that's kind.

Roshi didn't want anything when I called up the stairs to see if he needed his late afternoon hot water. As I closed the door, Russell said, quoting case #48, "I don't resent the amputation of my feet."

A lot of spiders today, inside and out, on snow, floating on the water in the toilet bowl. Fly in my room. Someone told me that the flies you see in the wintertime are always gravid females.

Angry fantasies of firing Roshi and seeing if Philip will have me for a student.

Candle on the altar went out spontaneously during evening zazen.

Mark is off for a three-day private retreat in someone's winter-abandoned yurt.

Her

My mother, Frimi, arrives. Isabel and I pick her up in Albuquerque. She is in an easy, pleasant mood. Room service at Inn at Loretto.

Sleep-over.

2.28.92
DATE

Him

Shikunichi.

Last day as doan.

Dream: Roshi pointedly rearranges some flowers I've placed in his room into a dramatic, but much more conventional, arrangement.

Apparently I forgot to include the Heart Sutra in English in the morning service. Roshi yelled from the top of the stairs, slamming his hand on the bannister: "You're the *INO*! You should know these things! The altar and the service are the one thing in the world that should be perfect! If you make an unavoidable mistake, that's okay, but I don't know why you do these things!"

Went back up (one of the few things I've ever learned is to keep showing up) offering hot water and flowers.

Roshi: "I'm sorry I've been getting so mad at you," then chastising me again. "You're angry at Gerald and Gisela, but if I put them in charge of Santa Fe they'd make it work. There's a way to practice that includes people."

2.29.92
DATE

"I'm not angry at Gerald and Gisela."

"Well, you put them down, and rightly so."

Told Gerald Roshi'd hammered me for the service, and he said, "But it's the only mistake you've made."

Lynne helped me fold Roshi's white kimono—very complicated. "Even if it's not right," I tell her, "I can redo it tomorrow. Today I'm working on guilt reduction."

"I often spend shikunichi doing that," she said.

Drove to Saguache with Russell after picking up our mail in Crestone. A sleepy town, poor like the rest of the valley. "Nebraska surrounded by mountains," says Russell. We agreed it wasn't as beautiful or mysterious as New Mexico, a subtle thing of color and texture of mountain and village life.

The Dinner Bell was full of Spanish people, also Robert Flagg, another shave-headed Zen monk, not from our lineage, and his blond girlfriend.

Sleepy-sad malaise.

Came back late, but walked with Gerald as arranged. Picked him up at his house, where he was discussing ice deposits on the roof with Larry and Gisela; "almost a triangle," as Steve said. From five to a little after seven we walked down to the stoneworks at the old gold mine and back, crunching loudly along the clean layer of snow left by the county plow. Pleasantries for a while, then he brought up what I'd said in staff meeting—we turned it over and over in the present, how could we work together, how to communicate, how to work off of the feeling of being Dharma brothers; also—Miriam, Roshi, Isabel, Gisela, Angelique (the hardest).

Miriam Bobkoff commanded me on the phone to take care of Gerald and Gisela.

Felt good, open and hopeful. Talked to Miriam.

Long bath and head shave in the tub 9:45–10:30 P.M.

Her

Wake up fun in hotel. Breakfast downstairs.

Mad shopping: Frimi buys me, at Chicos—dark apricot dress with tropical print vest, long and elegant. Buys Isabel:

puzzle of hands

puzzle of girl you put clothes on

two sets tiny dollies with playground, etc.

five tiny troll dolls

one musical turtle

Also, she brought an adorable baby doll who lives in a pink trunk with clothes.

All of these things a big hit. Isabel dotes on her.

Fenn Gallery sculpture garden with ducks.

Big party for my novel *Coastal Lives*—good time—fifty plus people—sell sixteen—Annie Baylor brings roses. Tom, Debora, Hope, Sabrina, Kath, and Sharon, in cute mini, X., who attacks my "extraneous use of detail" in a friendly way. N. tells me later in the car that she hears B. has a huge dick. Even later on the phone C. says that he kissed her once and was terrible.

Him

Dream: Reb and I are in a house that is San Francisco Zen Center. Baker-roshi is coming. The inhabitants of the house are anxious; they don't know what to do.

Doshi at morning service. Loosening my torso and including everyone.

Roshi is listening to a video on sleep research, and typing. I run up and down the stairs with teapots, flower scissors, breakfast tray, etc.

Sit in the atrium with Steve, who says he's in his most disturbed psychic state. Images of violence and "spiders exploding into young girls." He looks shrunken. Angel looks better, tousle-haired and gorgeous.

Steve on Roshi: "It's always like going into a room with a tiger. He tries to scare you away."

I am church mouse today, small and fleet of foot, hoping not to be noticed.

3.1.92
DATE

The roof is leaking where it's covered by tons of dirt.

Bright day, but overcast.

Roshi: "When is Miriam coming back? If she is coming back. I want to talk to you about the flower arrangement." He explains that I'm doing it wrong.

Gerald says he ran out of the zendo to write down what he was so angry about.

Afternoon house meeting. Didn't really say what I had to say—too quiet, too introverted, too inhibited, too late in the discussion. I didn't back Steve up. Could barely open my mouth. So hard to keep saying, "This is not okay." Bitterly ashamed after.

Her

Breakfast with a cheery Miriam Bobkoff, Isabel to Reuben's, nice ladies' lunch with Frimi at a very elegant Inn of the Anasazi, all sticks tied up in navy blue vases; tea with Debora and Gabriel; Frim behaves all of her visit. She and Isabel have a funny sparkly feeling in common; they are both a bit imperious.

An intense dream: my maternal grandparents are dead. Frimi takes me (us?) back to the old house. It is empty, but the longer we stay the more it fills up with familiar furniture, objects. An evil magician appears. He claims the house is his. I battle him. I wear horns and a crescent moon on my head. I feint his bursts of energy with my hands. He collapses, burned up.

3.1.92
DATE

Him

Dream: Holding a man, my employee, from behind under the arms. He's choking from having sipped a glass of water after talking to a strange woman. "It's not water," he says, and dies, despite my attempts to knock out what's obstructing his throat. The water is clear but heavy looking, like vodka. I set out in search of the woman.

Dogs howling around 10 P.M. and again in the morning dark.

Conversation with Roshi in Ulrike's room: "What are you worried about? No one's slapping you in the face."

I said, "The problem is, how healthy can it be to adapt to a sick and ailing community?"

He says one of the things that came between him and Steve was that Steve came to him with psychological explanations. The community isn't sick. Steve's trying too hard for the brown robe; he should, at his level of practice, be let to sink or swim, or be thrown into a pit of snakes and make dragons of them. (A mixed metaphor. In Chinese mythology, snakes don't become dragons, carp do. Dragons are Great Function monks. Snakes are trash.) He should enjoy the trees and sky, not get caught up in stuff. Angelique is "a powder keg." And so I shouldn't support Steve; he doesn't need it. Our disappearing into Steve and Angel's cabin after the meeting and coming late to dinner looked like a clique in an authoritarian power struggle.

I said it *was* an authoritarian power struggle, on the level of playground pushing, and I badly wanted out of it.

Roshi: "I don't want to see you get mired in this stuff. You took a position of authority in the meeting."

Ulrike, wearing a bathrobe, came in behind me while I was kneeling on the floor in front of Roshi and screamed. I put my hands over my head.

3.2.92
DATE

134

She said,"I hate it here." Later:"No, it's just that I have trouble with the practice."

I feel like some character with a tragic flaw, weak, divided, caught between my earnest desire to practice with Roshi, not to argue with him, and my feeling and understanding, which are clear enough but seem to have no place here. Hard not to internalize the denial. I'm sticking to an arbitrary boundary—if Steve and Angel leave, I'm out.

Ulrike left for Germany without saying good-bye.

Her

Talking to Robert on the phone is depressing and enervating. Crestone seems so dysfunctional.

Teach two private lessons, make $57.50 plus a set of new tarot-like cards, "Deepening" ones by Mary Rose. Card of a hole in the ground, a nest or that terrible hole in the Japanese horror movie full of the bones of samurai.

3.2.92 DATE

Him

Last night and this morning was doshi although Steve was in the zendo.

Coyotes ululating in the mountains during zazen.

I can feel my heart going out of this. I could do it, but why? While I'm not particularly angry now, I can see that later I would be; I'm at the limit of what I can process. If I leave, I'd like not to just move over to the next mountain and scream curses back here. I don't want *out,* don't want to go home; I want to move forward; I want to practice as a Zen person. I'd like to finish this practice period, then reevaluate my relationship with Roshi. I'd like to see Philip. I'd like to keep some kind of moral and emotional integrity.

Nothing much happening today: photocopy, fix, snow.

Steve and Angel left just before lunch for four days.

**3.3.92
DATE**

With Roshi in Denver, I'm the senior monastic officer, I think.

Staff meeting:

Sitting in Gerald and Gisela's house thinking, "This seems so reasonable"—is a lie.

"We expressed our feelings and they left—just like Joan."

Lynne is going to these staff meetings as bookkeeper. Mark seemed annoyed when I asked.

Fought with Miriam on the phone—she's denying that we ever arranged to let anyone stay. She doesn't want Steve and Angel coming to the house. I was angry, completely freaked, and cried—she's treating me like the enemy.

Called Fred, our therapist. He suggested—*1.* confronting Roshi—*2.* screaming at a tree in the woods.—*3.* kindness to Miriam—Says yes,

136

this is emotional abuse. "You were trained for this—secrets and abuse—by your family."

Her

Lovely creative process class with edit femmes. Wrote three rounds and then soaked in a hot tub!

Terrible blowout with Robert on the phone. Misunderstanding about hospitality re: Steve and Angel, but he feels I am lying to him, and cries, which breaks my heart. We work it out, but I just feel how devastating the situation is.

Later—Robert talks to Fred, who says the situation in the monastery is emotionally abusive. I love Robert, and miss him. I just feel battered. Decide to take a day at home and not go up until Thursday.

**3.3.92
DATE**

Him

Dream: Making love with Lizzie Grey. Reading a letter to ex-girlfriend Kathy from her mother detailing why her trust money is being increased; looking in it for clues to Kathy's whereabouts. Later, kissing Kathy.

Still doshi. Brief shikunichi morning zazen and service.

Snowing last night and this morning—thick fall, no wind.

Dennis promises pizza for breakfast.

Lynne: "No coffee 'til after soji."

Don: "What's that in the greenhouse?"

"Don't drink that. That's Gisela's coffee enema."

3.4.92
DATE
Built a fire in Roshi's room, filled his hot water thermos, in anticipation of his return. Miriam's put off returning a day on account of her mental state and the snow. Atrium and the office are flooded and the back part of the house is dark and cold—thin gray light through the snow on the skylights.

Reading poems Lyn Lifshin sent for *Fish Drum*.

BEER with the pizza at breakfast.

Snow up to the knees.

Roshi came back bearing a new community VCR from the Price Club.

My sister Julie says that she and I and our sister Suzi all have the same scenario—going into difficult fields; the garment industry, theater, hating it, but being unwilling to quit unless we'd gotten our own way. She said, "If you have trouble talking to him, visualize him in his underwear. It sounds like he's been taking advantage. You don't have to go for divorce; you could just get a separation. You're done. You've done what you needed to do. Just think of him as an old garmento whose neuroses and weird ideas are keeping him from making a million dollars."

Slept early afternoon. Dream: Young boy is fishing at King's Pond. He snags his hook. I'm laboriously reeling it in, pulling the rod tip back and reeling it forward along the line. It goes under a broad red ribbon running under the surface of the water. A man tries to dissuade or distract me. Ominous feelings. I stop several times, but know what I'll find—a Ping-Pong table, the one my father destroyed in a fit of rage when I was in my early teens. "Zen's red thread," the blood lineage I'm ordained in.

Roshi and I talked for an hour, half of it standing in front of the cappuccino machine in his bathroom drinking coffee. I managed to say most of what was on my mind in a clear way. What a struggle to be able to say, "Yes, I can see you think that, but I disagree." I told him I'd pegged my staying to Steve's because it avoided deciding all the time—an arbitrary boundary. He said, "But that would be the end of our relationship. I mean, I would think that was a ridiculous decision." I said, "Yes, I know."

3.4.92
DATE

I told him I felt that when the community left off being hostile, he'd started, and that the message seemed to be, if you want to play with the big boys, you can't have any loyalties other than to me—you have to obey, be hard, unemotional, play by my rules. He wanted to know, "Who are the big boys?" I said, "You're a big boy."

He said, "You have a capacity for staying in uncomfortable situations." Life in monasteries was often crazy; we were brought together by circumstances—if we couldn't create harmony here, then what good were we in the world? My saying, "This is a sick and ailing community," made the shoe fit, and needed to be worked out in other ways.

He said that I have a personality good for priesthood; things were problematic for me and I worked them out, and so could become a kind and aware priest, while someone like Reb took to it like a duck to water, was too perfect; it was too much of a career. Gerald was in line for dharma transmission and, further on, so was I.

Shitting blood.

Her

A tiny bit of snow coats everything, and a low white sky. Actually go to the plaza for coffee, Isabel in school. I decided I would treat myself well today, and try to relax. I feel heartbroken. This is like the breakup of San Francisco Zen Center all over again, and it isn't even my problem.

3.4.92
DATE Heartbreaking Brazilian music in Häagen-Dazs. I haven't written a poem in weeks, just articles, journal, and my mouth glued to the icy kiss of novel revision that won't let go.

Fantasies of cancer, fantasies of suicide—mostly when I am at the monastery. Fantasies of divorce, fantasies of harm come to Isabel. I can't live with this hole in my life much longer.

Polyrhythm. Café au lait. The things I don't know. I guess I really do love Robert, something I haven't felt this profoundly in several months. I felt it when he cried.

Steve and Angel arrive after lunch, looking dazed. Isabel sent home from day care with diarrhea, but seems okay. Take her to the mall, carousel, library. Nice takeout dinner from Dave's with Steve and Angelique; watch *The Lion in Winter*.

Him

Morning meeting with Roshi. Do I trust him enough to go further? Snow fell several times with a bang and stuck to the window—Roshi said it was melting off the roof—when I went downstairs Russell told me it was he and Olaf throwing snowballs to see if they could get a rise out of us.

Roshi: "If you think I'm angry at you because of other situations, I can't trust you." He also said some of the energy came from these other situations; students at Zen Center colluded behind his back, etc.; that I'm not open, raw—I hear and understand what he's teaching but adjust it to fit to a greater or lesser extent.

Staff meeting—I'm careful, general, mildly critical. Roshi asked me to withdraw my energy from these problems, to speak personally and not for others, and to support the situation. My view of it is quite harsh, but I have withdrawn, by concentrating on my relationship with Roshi.

3.5.92
DATE

Notebooks come out during seminar when Roshi explains "hair-blown sword"—same three that heard it the day before from me.

Letter from Tom: Isabel tells him, "Angelique has a tiny house."

Her

Angel makes cappuccino—tease them—homeless monks with cappuccino machine. Steve looks terrible, haggard.

Leave 9 A.M. Hazy drive, bits of snow, rain, clear, big mist, fog. Robert drives down beyond the bridge to meet us. Takes us up in four-wheel drive. Long nap with Isabel. Date with Robert in Steve and Angelique's cabin. It's cold. We're warm. Robert says he has to decide about Baker-roshi. I don't understand all the parameters. He still needs to yell at a tree. Some sense he can't verbalize it because it isn't verbal. I'm through with the people here, so-called community. I think they are sick. I think they can't change. I think they just aren't my problem.

3.5.92
DATE

Him

Roshi left zazen during second period so I'm still doshi at service. Took Isabel to work meeting.

Now that Isabel can pee in the pot, we'll save about $500 a year and also ecological-landfill guilt on diapers.

"You don't have to serve me," says Isabel.

"What does that mean?" I ask.

"I don't know."

Don: "I was married to a screamer for fifteen years." She was Japanese.

Instead of lunch, hiked up the mountain to the stream through snow coming up a little over my knees; spread a tarp in front of a big aspen, knelt, saw it as rooted, hard to hurt—Roshi—and yelled and broke four sticks on it. Not very articulate: "Bullshit," "That's not okay," "Selective memory," "Social climber."

3.6.92
DATE

Miriam: "What do you want in your heart of hearts?"

Me: "I want to spend time with Philip before he dies."

Miriam: "I'm sorry I asked. Just pretend he's dead."

Isabel was tired and cranky as we three walked down the road, stopping and going the other way several times, crying and refusing to come. I asked her how she felt.

"I feel sad."

"Why?"

"I want you to miss me."

A knot of feeling dissolves during evening zazen.

Her

Wake up feeling a bit claustrophobic. Robert is nice to me.
Finger-paint and animal stamps with Isabel.
Work:
Update financial part of ledger
Sell bond
Write only draft of *Reporter* article "No Frills" house decorating
Write two stanzas "Beauty and Beast"
Revise "Jacob and Angel" poem
Get phone messages
Tidy room
Laundry? Where is it?
Gerald says he wants to talk to me. I could go to the house meeting, but should I?

3.6.92
DATEMy common sense says: stay away. My killer instinct: go.

Susannah calls—tells me she is pregnant! Thrilling, but a bit scary, because of the risk, ectopic, etc.

House meeting. Robert and I decide for political reasons that I should go. Steam rising from a pot of tea, a white pot.

The topic: Steve and Angelique.

A kind of soft discussion, the door is open, etc.

Then—we hate Steve. He was mean to us.

Dennis is brilliant, if vague, takes the traditional approach; you have to ask a teacher to teach, etc.

Gisela and Lynne had their feelings hurt. Gerald refuses to talk because he has hurt other people's feelings.

"The situation with Rufus (the dog) has changed. Don't feed the black cat Zafu."

Him

Dokusan: Roshi says he's tired of telling me these things—we're friendly but not friends, and if he never saw me again but I did each thing precisely for the rest of my life, he'd feel it was a successful relationship. Reminded me again that I hadn't sewn my robes on time—to hear the thrust of what he was saying, not the details. Listen. Take it to heart. Or we didn't have a relationship. I should've resigned as ino in Santa Fe if I was going to be late. I have to do things thoroughly. The anja work was not being done thoroughly, etc.

When I brought up breakfast I resigned as anja. "I didn't mean for you to resign," he said. I'd considered what I could handle, and ino-ing and Isabel were it. I'll continue to bring water and whatnot. Helped him make his bed. Roshi says, "You have to always put the quilt back on the bed the same way or you spend the nights smelling feet."

Isabel watches intently while I take off my robes.

"Do you think all dads have robes?" I ask.

"Some do and some don't," she says.

She waits for me to roll up my *obi* (kimono belt) so she can put the clip on. Put on a nightgown and kick off my underwear.

"Are you going to sleep without any underwear on your vagina? I have pull-ups on because I pee at night."

Tell her that I have a penis; and when you're small and when you're very old you pee at night, but when you're middle-aged, you usually don't. Miriam says from her sleep, "But I do."

Her

Menstrual period.
Robert quits as anja.
Nice talk with Gerald.
Isabel is pretty much potty trained these days.
Feel happy, but don't know why.
Write poems all afternoon.

3.7.92
DATE

Him

Doshi again. Turned over assembly and delivery of Roshi's breakfast to Gerald as breakfast cook, and can therefore take the break after breakfast, then do soji. Showered in the break—funny how much it affects the background of my feelings and sense of well-being to be clean.

Roshi laid claim to the phrase "The work of sleep is done in zazen."

Isabel: "Are you reading a book about sitting zazen?"

Roshi: "The ino's job is to lead the chanting. To be present in the zendo. The sutra card should be right in front of me. Why didn't you put it there?"

"I thought..."

"It's not your job to think."

3.8.92
DATE

Her

Go to Saguache with Robert and Isabel for lunch. East of Moffat, straight across the valley, cold mountains and flat plain, beginning to warm up, ditches of water and red salt cedars. Robert astounds me by saying first that it looks like Atlantic City, and then claiming it looks just like New Jersey if you ignore the mountains. These mountains are difficult to ignore. Lunch at the Dinner Bell—a New Mexico-feeling greasy spoon. Eat a baked potato with meat and cheese. Play in the simple little park, mud and tree roots, Isabel ecstatic on the swing as Robert pushes her higher. On the way home, Robert sinks the car in mud on the soft shoulder of the road. Almost immediately a truck appears with chain and pulls us out. Later, it snows; I have diarrhea, feeling like a touch of flu, chills. Fine by morning.

3.8.92
DATE

Saguache is the kind of life you can't really imagine, despite the family out on Sunday bicycles and the way those big mountains make you feel; they are so cold and remote, and they don't give birth, the way the sea does, and they don't hide treasure: diatoms, wrecks, pearls. Still, you can't imagine what the waitress with purple-dyed hair is really doing there. Like all life it feels repetitive, precious, irrelevant. People get cancer and have babies, plant irises, get divorced. I will never cease to wonder. The county seat means you can get a marriage license, or a library card. Trucks stop for an hour, a day. This is America. I asked Robert if we would always think every place was provincial because we were born in Manhattan. He says: New York City is very provincial.

Him

Shikunichi. Ran into Steve and Angelique, Lynne, and Dennis in town. The three women ahead of me at the post office each had packages waiting for them, needed stamps and a money order, had lots of outgoing mail, hadn't brought the key to their boxes, and asked Monty to get their mail (despite a sign refusing that service).

Watched *Problem Child* with Isabel twice. *Stand & Deliver* with Miriam, Isabel, Angel, and recently arrived Daniel (Miriam's brother) and Alisa (his girlfriend).

Her

Off day. Big breakfast. Steve and Angel are back, look okay. Daniel and Alisa due to arrive. Drawings and stickers with Isabel. Sunshine on snow.

3.9.92
DATE

Him

No wake-up bell. Can't remember telling Dennis he was it, just that I thought it was taken care of for the last two days. Went up at the break and resigned as ino—Roshi said, "But you're concentrating on it," and refused, accepted an apology instead and said Dennis as doan should apologize to me.

Steve: "...[they] think that she's just here as my wife."

Roshi: "That's a sexist remark."

Lynne: "It's one of the more useful sexist remarks."

Gisela: "They took everything out so she cannot receive babies."

Cyclamen.

Isabel: "Hoops mean fire and fire means tickle you! Ha ha ha ha!"

Long walk with Daniel, Alisa, Isabel to Gerald and Gisela's house, past Steve and Angelique's, studio, dome, Don's, stomping through the snow to Joan's yurt, Daniel and Alisa bickering ahead, and I, carrying Isabel. Daniel left for a nap and Alisa and I went way down the road and back just in time for lunch.

3.10.92
DATE

Long talk with Roshi in the evening after I brought tea.

Went by Daniel and Alisa's open door and saw Miriam cross-legged on the bed, Daniel and Alisa under the covers, talking about art. Miriam: "The way you make a living from your art is to do it for fifteen years without making a living."

Her

Blow job under the sheets last night.

Daniel and Alisa here.

Write a chapter, letters, etc.

Sex date.

Stay up late talking—about fears of being an artist, fear of failure. I feel sympathetic, but on some level just don't get it. I never really felt that way.

Him

Roshi: "I'm telling you these things because at a certain point the student needs to be able to see things from the teacher's point of view. Not that you have to agree. You can both agree and disagree.... I feel you accept what I say, but you don't see it the way I do.... Stand both firmly in your own shoes and in other people's."

Looking for "we are such stuff as dreams are made on," for Roshi. Wishing for Bartlett's, and sure, along with Miriam and Mark, that it's in *A Midsummer Night's Dream*. Check *Romeo and Juliet*. Wondering where else there are fairies. Found it in *The Tempest*.

Dennis: "By and large, I feel very misunderstood."

Don: "The possibility of being misunderstood is very high."

3.11.92
DATE

Her

Work in A.M., then go home, meet Alisa and Danny in Alamosa for caravan.

Dream: I am single and must date. Put on purple silk dress and put my hair up in a ponytail. A very bad feeling.

Him

Roshi in Santa Fe. Left me with laundry, photocopying.

Gisela's going for a week; I'll be guest master. She booked a student into my room even though there are two open. "We don't have students by themselves. Don't you want to get to know him?" I put him in Randy's empty room, telling her, "He can get to know Dennis and Russell."

The two-by-sixes that hold up the plank ceiling in the laundry room are bowed, and one is cracked crosswise. Tomorrow someone'll have to shovel off some of the dirt roof and shore up the beams from underneath.

Napped in the afternoon and dreamed I was singing a sentimental ballad with Poetry Devils—I asked a woman if she liked it; she hated it, not understanding the irony. I repressed the urge to tell her it was okay to hate it.

3.12.92
DATE

Her

Thursday at home. Isabel to day care, spend hours on the phone catching up, get an offer of two weeks work from Prep. Daniel and Alisa baby-sit; teach in the evening.

Him

Doshi. Conferred with Steve, who said he's given up and is looking for a graceful exit. Taught Olaf beginning bells and drums so he can be doan. Roshi's laundry is streaked with detergent—will have to wash again. Talked to sister Suzi last night. Dreamed I was out to eat with two blondes who were kissing each other; one was Loren. Drove to Salida to pick up guest student arriving by Greyhound, which was an hour late. Read Philip's poetry.

Her

Walk the studio site. Daniel and I nervous when I set limits about money. But Alisa has a good intuition about how to explain. We settle tentatively on a rectangle with a little jag in it, freestanding.

Coffee with Carol. Isabel cranky, takes a long bath. Drive to Albuquerque with Tom—both of us tense before we read, a crowd of about forty at the Living Batch. Tom reads great stuff about Poland, Ania washing windows on Holy Week. Strange feeling of fear on the highway, the car does not feel substantial, dirty windshield. Alisa breaks her string of jade beads and puts them in the blue milk pitcher.

3.13.92
DATE

Him

Shikunichi. Doshi, though Roshi was there. I was waiting at my seat, just beginning to wonder why he was taking so long to get to the bowing mat, when he quietly called my name. So I performed in front of him, then awkwardly proceeded him out of the zendo. He critiqued it after we bowed together in front of his door. Bowing was too fast, and I should touch my head three times with each bow. Walking was too slow, not powerful enough. Should be on two axes—vertical, holding still in place, and horizontal, pulling forward from the stomach as if right through the wall, with feet sliding, not lifted. Step back off the mat entirely for the second bow, not just backward.

Couldn't get any privacy today—someone knocked on my door every few minutes. Roshi had errands.

3.14.92
DATE
Russell and I escaped to Saguache and went to the library. New calves in the fields. One just born, steaming, its mother licking it. Calves sitting just outside the fences. Dead striped skunk, a big one. Coyote running across the road in the Baca.

Ran into Steve on the road who at first I thought was sunburned, then realized was glowing with anger. "How are you?" I asked. "Enraged," he said. "I've been walking along being enraged. Shouting at the rocks."

Lay in bed reading. Stomachache kept me up late.

Her

How odd to say I'll miss going to the monastery.

A Mayumi Oda goddess, small and white, hiding under the big green lily pads, breasts pointing down. Three Minoan goddesses, curvy, hanging on a reproduced plaque to the right of the desk. Robert says I love objects; but sometimes I ignore them. Alisa says she neglects her clothes for graduate school, but she has a jacket with huge buttons. Carol looks beautiful as always in her captured-gypsy outfits. If I am very depressed or sick I don't wear earrings. Debora needs to feel all right to dress— witness the year of the basketball sneakers. Hope has her own chic. Miriam Bobkoff wears only navy blue, a fetishist.

Tea with the Lambs, and many cookies—as pleasant as always.

Gabriel's first birthday party—easygoing and happy. Isabel and Reuben play extensively on the stairs. Return Gabriel's umbilical cord, which had been in our freezer for a year, to his parents.

3.14.92
DATE

Trouble with the wall. Back neighbors are renovating, seem to have loosened the quadrant nearest to their shed. They are rude and imply it is somehow all my fault. Just the top seems loose. It will fall onto our side, but are we somehow responsible? I'll get Danny to take a look. They want us to go in on the cost of the coyote fence, but Robert says no. The neighbor gives a bad impression; he storms, "I am an architect." I asked them to remove the loose stone, but they did not. They have agreed to cart the rubble away, rubble on our side.

Him

Doshi, then instructed Don and returned to bed after service. Dog barking outside during zazen wasn't Janie. Dreamed I was skating around a residential neighborhood in zori slippers, happy though viewed with scorn by the neighborhood children. I tried to teach them to skate, not walk, but they didn't care to listen.

Lay in bed and read *G Is for Gumshoe* and *Star Patrol,* which had that familiar Andre Norton flavor—outdoor alien gothic, a little gray, but absorbing. Realized near the end I'd read it before.

Sat evening zazen.

Her

3.15.92
DATE

Bad dream about the ocean, dead fish, high waves, no showers. I am with Isabel, or a slightly older child. Also have to wipe a woman's shit in a somewhat sexual situation—it is actually a box of shit.

Sunday morning, 8:30 A.M., Isabel sleeps, I drink coffee in bed, desperately try to finish reading overdue Leslie Marmon Silko book.

Nice visit with Mei-Mei and Martha, walk in the park, although Isabel throws a fit when we leave. Mei-Mei in her yellow sweater and black leggings looks like the bumblebee hand puppet she holds.

Lunch with Daniel and Alisa. Alisa goes to San Francisco. Isabel cranky.

Him

Morning zazen, then back to bed. Not very tired, or sick, just head and stomach ache. Slept a little. Awakened by Roshi about 10:30 from dream that Mir was giving me a blow job in the kitchen. Lay in bed and felt wonderful for a while, listening to preparations in the kitchen for wedding this afternoon and dinner after. Kamala the Indian dancer and the prospective husband arrived yesterday.

Steller's jays outside the window.

Miriam called; Bruce Lamb, who grew up just outside this valley, told her the farmers' problem is that they never demineralized the artesian water for irrigating, and the soil is ruined. Talked to Isabel, asking her if she'd had fun with Mei-Mei's daughter. Isabel: "She name is Martha, right?" Miriam says the two children are much of a muchness, "precise and stubborn."

Angelique came by and told me about a vision quest with Joan in the desert, "full of Death-Mother energy." We talked about dope and driving in cars and cops.

3.16.92
DATE

Can feel things resolve in zazen sometimes, an almost-physical shift of acceptance. I can see my way toward the end of the practice period. Leaving Roshi, if I decide to then, will be all right.

Miriam said she'd dreamed she was fucking Roshi while trying to make tea. Angel said she had dreams he was fucking her in the ass, "like the thief distracts you while he's robbing you in the koan." Told her hers was the ass-fucking lineage, remembering how Steve said lineages have their own karma, and he could feel it put on with the robe.

Went into the kitchen to score some lunch around 2:30. Russell said I was "frighteningly cheerful." Slept around 3:30, while the *densho* bell was signaling the beginning of the wedding ceremony. Woke around 7:00, while dinner was being had: champagne corks opening.

Her

Busy Monday. No school. Errands. Sharon at the *Reporter* lets Isabel play on the computer, likes my stories. Greg and Reuben for lunch. Turns out Greg knows the back neighbors. I have already delivered note about liability that my insurance agent suggested. All is friendly—they'll jerry-rig the wall. Obviously men understand this, and women do not. Talk about study—frame? adobe? block? I begin to be able to see it.

Kath and Miriam Bobkoff for dinner, out for ice cream on the plaza.

Paul Mishler called! He'd found and read my poetry book—*True Body*. Very emotional to talk to him…happy…but then I cried in the car…cried for all the intensity I felt when I was thirteen years old. Combined with that letter from Richard Feldman (I went to summer camp with both of them), the past is heating up, and something is about to come due.

3.16.92
DATE

Him

Doshi. Cleaned zendo for soji, then went to talk with Roshi. Resigned as his student, saying that I wanted to leave, but I wanted to do it in a way so that I'd be welcome back. Roshi agreed, asking that I stay through sesshin, and on as ino. Said I was thorough and sensitive in a good way, but that everything had an emotional charge for me. That he'd been impeccable as a teacher, though harder on me than anyone. I was startled, asked if he was kidding. Says I'm making a mistake in terms of practice, though perhaps not personally. Asked me to practice precision, no dissonance of language and action.

Roshi: "What is a Zen master?"

Me: "Someone whose mind is in accord with reality in a low-down kind of way."

Roshi: "Yes, but it's not enough. If it's just that, and the situation is a mess, then your mind is a mess. The archetype is, someone whose mind is not disturbed no matter what."

3.17.92
DATE

Me: "How about Vimalakirti? He was sick because of the suffering of all sentient beings."

Roshi: "I don't know. A Zen master resides in his sense fields, with no 'out there.'"

Worked on Roshi's kobaku box instead of lunch, which I ate late. Veggie sushi, delicious.

Took a nap. Dreamed that Arnie Kotler (a dharma brother) and I were walking toward each other to hug, each limping, he from a wound in his leg, me from one in my foot.

Mark stuck his head in the door to ask if I was making dinner as the alarm went off. I washed the dishes after, while most of the place went off to watch Kamala dance at Sarah's.

159

Heard the husband singing at the table after dinner, something I've only ever heard people do in New York. They are from New York. Came through the open casement window as I sat drinking champagne in jelly glasses with Angel. Told Russell I hated neoclassical improv—he said I probably hadn't heard the growly nonmusical flesh-slapping parts, being too far away. Turns out the singer was Tom Buckner, and my opin-ion improved—the record I have of his is pretty okay.

Her

Edit femmes writing group.

Lunch with Hope and a cranky set of Isabel, Reuben, and Dylan. Isabel climbs the big hill behind the house, clambering strongly after the big boys.

3.17.92 DATE Robert calls and says he has quit Baker-roshi, is no longer his student. I feel good for Robert, who has done something he needed to do, but sad about it too—this scene has been part of our lives from the first. But I don't feel panicky—this is Robert's decision after all, and his life. I just tell him I am not moving from Santa Fe. I guess the fat man (Philip Whalen) is next on the agenda. Next on my agenda is a few months of family normalcy. I feel very relieved that Robert won't still be running the zendo here in some capacity—his routine has not seemed to be working in the past year. But I respect his being a monk and want him to stay one—can't see us satisfied just by an ordinary life: house, profession, child. There has to be intention underneath, and wildness.

We'll see...last August I felt a cycle was over, my life would change. Maybe some big change is brewing.

Him

Elizabeth, Miriam, and Isabel arrive during seminar. I make some tea, settle them in. Isabel and I sing and make goldfish faces in the bathroom without realizing the sound is carrying down the halls of the monastery. She sings a three-year-old's song over and over, "I have no more paa-tience with you my daar-ling. I will kill you..." When she's asleep, Miriam and I go into the shower room and fuck on the floor.

Her

Will drive to Crestone with Russell's Elizabeth.

Errands, clean house, put cute clothes on layaway at Margo's.

Think about Robert, of course, and what will happen next...I realized yesterday, I love it here. Santa Fe is my place. This house is my house.

3.18.92
DATE

Him

Wake up feeling blissed out and with a hard-on.

Roshi sits in his seat, and I officiate at service. It's getting easier to stay in the groove while he's around—I move from the belly, as if I might plow through the wall. Steve said, "I know how to do macho Zen practice. You take your energy and ram it through your asshole into the ground."

Shikunichi.

Elizabeth, Russell, Isabel, and I drive to town in Miriam's Toyota. We talk about fiction in the car. Elizabeth is writing a novel in the style of Edith Wharton. Russell and I've been in the monastery so long that, though we both work in a library, we can't remember any too well what books are, or what we've read.

3.19.92
DATE Drive south along mountains to the bird sanctuary: flat fields hacked out of gray-green sage, some standing water, cottonwood windbreaks and salt cedar. Two flocks of sandhill cranes purring and clacking, also a pair of whooping cranes, not full-grown but head and shoulders above the sandhills. Isabel and I run down the road flapping our arms, yelling, "Fly! Fly!"

Isabel pees on a side road—pulls up her pants and takes off, running flat out. Prairie falcon bolts out of a cottonwood. Isabel: "A DINO-SAUR caught me! A DINOSAUR caught me!"

We stop at the alligator farm, a roofed hot spring where they raise alligators and tilapia. Isabel and I were here when she was a year old. The alligators stood and walked forward, expecting to be fed, and baby Isabel reared back and hissed at them with her arms spread.

Our guide is about four feet tall, and holds onto her breasts the whole time, shivering. Isabel decides that she wants to stay "for a couple weeks." When she recounts her adventures later she remembers the alligators, but it's mostly about "the little girl. She was bigger than me."

Her

Sex in the bathroom in the middle of the night. Down on my knees sucking Robert's cock. Wake up at 4 A.M., hip joints out from fucking on concrete floor. Take two Advil.

Monastery thoughts: A young woman with a broken-down car is a completely different creature from a young woman with a fancy car. A young woman with a Toyota truck is a dyke, or on her own, or both.

Errands—why do people complain about them. "Oh," they say, "I have so many errands." And then, ominously: and I have to keep the house clean. Miriam Bobkoff has the fewest errands of anyone. I am also the kind of person who throws out old shoes, much as I love the smell of the shoe repair store. What I have are phone calls—terrible messages of students and divorce, ectopic pregnancies, and fiscal disaster, which I must return at once, or else.

Him

Roshi didn't show for zazen, so I bowed us in, sat down, and mostly slept between bouts of meditation. Dream: man sitting in an open suitcase full of water says, "Should I go or could I stay here?" Led service, then hissed at the director that I was going to bed. Heard Roshi talking to Isabel while I was sleeping. "Were you up a lot in the night?" "No, just to pee."

Lower eyelid is swollen and sore today so I call the doctor in Moffat, leave Isabel with Miriam during work period, and drive over. Have hordeolum, an inflamed gland or duct. Bill is $31 including meds, which I borrow from Miriam.

Elizabeth has gone back to Santa Fe with Angel. It's good Angel got out of here; yesterday she was walking around after her shower with her hair up in a towel, vibrating with rage, saying, "I know where the gun is. I'm just going to take a shotgun and blow those two assholes away." The two assholes being Roshi and Gerald. She and I both take comfort in knowing that people underestimate how vicious we're willing to be. Just 'cause we're usually polite doesn't mean we won't revert to the street. It's wildly inappropriate for a pair of priests.

Gerald and Gisela and some guests arrive after lunch. Gisela began to put away chairs; Mark told her we'd decided to leave them out for dinner, the contractors were coming. "Oh yes?" she said, and continued to put them away.

Her

Ordinary, slightly boring monastery day.

Bad night—moonlight, dogs, propane leak. Isabel up every hour, weird dreams.

Robert to doctor for his infected eye. Didn't work in the morning. Fun visit at Angel's—pretzels, dancing to reggae, a computer program with flowing stream and croaking frogs that does a kind of I-ching throw.

Work in afternoon. Actually finish novel, but this is not as momentous as it sounds, all tiny bits add up. Ideas for future—holocaust poem. Robert said it is hard to think/write about because it is, on one level, a large/abstract event.

Baker-roshi tells me to move my car right before dinner. Bundle Isabel up, do it, miss the start of dinner, Isabel cranky, a general feeling that nothing works and I don't like it here. Eat in the room.

3.20.92
DATE

Him

Dream I've been incarcerated for a year and a half of a six-year sentence in a crawl space under the floor of a house. It's not too onerous; I just sit zazen, lying on my back with my arms at my sides. The air is thick and stale. Go see Philip perform—he's reading in a restaurant, doing his Pillsbury Doughboy dance at the microphone, and singing his poems. It's wonderful.

Doshi.

Zazen: "Death going to pounce on your head."

Room smells of propane from the leaky heater.

Isabel and I go to Saguache, trade in books at the library, pick up new ones, and use the bathroom four times while we play in the playground next door. Slide using waxed paper, something I knew only from hearsay. Swing for an hour. "Higher! Push me higher! Now upside down! The little girl flying through the air! The child is flying through the air! You can't catch me, you can't catch me, because I'm far away!" She's really heartbreakingly beautiful today, her face flushed, hair blown in tangles, Japanese coat. The librarian, like everyone else, remarks on her cuteness.

3.21.92
DATE

Elaborate Chinese lunch from Robert Flagg.

Staff meeting. Don relates that Dennis wants to do the garden this summer, not just to work in but to have charge of it. Lynne is disgusted. "If these people who've been practicing for many years are like this, then what are we to think," though he's asking for a domain, any domain, which she'd once been desperate to have. Talking about a pottery studio, Gisela unveils her plan to cut Dennis's room in half and use that space (and his only window) for potting.

Blow job from Mir, late, after much talk.

Her

Isabel is really on the rampage, no to everything. Robert takes her to Saguache to play, and she returns in a far mellower mood.

M., a local lady, brings her son by to play with Isabel. She is forty, the widow of a famous psychologist who had ten children, some her age. She wears yellow-green velveteen heels in the mud, and says: "I was living with the Shah of Iran's brother-in-law, at that level, you know, when the revolution broke out." She is from New Zealand; and now because the will is contested she is "penniless." After a chat she absconds to have coffee with Baker-roshi, leaving me with the kids, which I did not mind, as the little boy was "sweet," as Isabel said, and they played nicely.

Compare her to Z. How women end up with children but no money. How women hope men will save them. How women just don't plain think. Women on the edge of the jet set who end up with a Cartier watch and some good jewelry—no house, no profession, no investments, no husband, just the usual children. Compare this to your average waitress. M. cooks brunch for a living, teaches yoga, in a town of a hundred. These women can work hard, or, more accurately, they can survive, but at a minimum level, without rich men. They will never write a book, but they will always have great clothes—left over from a previous life with some shah's brother-in-law—they will always be thin, and they will never wear costume jewelry, because the holes in their ears are allergic.

3.21.92
DATE

When his father died, the son was a year and a half old. He stopped eating, is still a bit small.

Robert says, unsympathetically, that this kind of lady is just a groupie, that ladies everywhere do this dependency number in some fashion. But does it actually *work*? People give them houses, cars, but they are terrible drivers. It's a better life than being an unloved Albuquerque housewife;

at least it has some edge. People don't give me cars and houses. People give me garbage bags full of zucchini, rhinestone earrings, children's books, gigs, and trust funds.

Him

Doshi.

Have 4 and 9 day-type breakfast for architect Bruce King, and discuss the siting of the new zendo. Roshi: "Look for motion and stillness. Stick your finger in the dirt. A mountain behind and one to either side to make a seat. A mountain, a valley, running water. Where the plants and animals do well—we can take a place and improve it, unlike a Tao-ist approach, just finding the best place. The mountain behind the altar. See it nonconceptually. Luminous light…currents."

**3.22.92
DATE**

More at ease here not being Roshi's student. No big changes yet. Been avoiding him just a little by not making any effort to see him; I'm sure it shows.

Propane ran out—no stove, hot water, heat. Electricity may be hashing machines again. Both TVs and VCR on the fritz.

Isabel and I are insanely cranky. Miriam's suddenly boundaryless and won't back off.

168

Her

Some snow in the morning, leaky smell of propane—Robert says heater needs to be on, with window open, to not leak. Stupid system. Isabel tells me a long story or dream in which two bad guys are given two cows to eat, presumably instead of people, and then Gisela appears carrying a large fish.

Blow job under the covers last night.

Run out of propane. Basically a crabby day. Isabel cranky. Finally take her to lunch at the Road Kill—I have a fine hamburger; she has a large bowl of vanilla ice cream with sprinkles.

Robert snaps at me twenty times. No heat. Okay evening with Isabel—stories and songs. She loves the story of David and Goliath and asks uncannily: "What does David sing?"

3.22.92
DATE

Him

Dream: one of several chunky guys in a suit fucks someone and leaves after calling in an air strike.

Doshi.

Roshi is perturbed that I've spoken about our breakup. I wanted to have some overt process with the residents as well, and told him so.

Take Isabel to POA library, Moffat post office, Saguache playground.

Flocks of blackbirds on the road, bluebirds, crows, a magpie.

One of the secret pleasures of parenthood is reexperiencing some of one's own childhood. It's a minor thing, but driving with Isabel across the fields, they came alive for me out of my own past, leaf mold smell, white flowers in the sage, wild wet secrets under the overcast sky, and animals to find close to the ground, among the reeds, in the grass and water. Seeing white flowers in the salt cedar too made me realize I was seeing clumps of snow, nearsightedly.

3.23.92
DATE

Her

Overcast, snowy, and chill without heat in the house.

Long dream about spending several hours in a museum. Also, dream in which I am reading a story by Kath about a murder or a deathbed scene. Some jealous spouse implications. Baker-roshi is in the story. I explain how he would really act. Kath gets furious and says something like "they didn't tell me" (the other people in the group).

Him

Dream: SB commits suicide.

Shikunichi.

Drive to Salida for lunch with Miriam and Isabel.

Her

Go to Salida for lunch. Isabel is horribly cranky, and slams car door on her father. Nice talk in the car with Robert.

3.24.92
DATE

Him

Dream: cutting off the bottom of some wooden bowls while my father complains.

Pack my extra stuff and load car while Mir lies down. Isabel's been pesky, but sits on the curb, watches quietly, and drinks her milk. They leave midmorning.

Staff meeting. Gerald introduces a plan to put a hydroelectric generator under Don's cabin.

Her

Go home. Isabel wretched—bossy, cranky, whining, sobbing. I yell. Come home and unload the car in a huge fit of anger.

3.25.92
DATE

172

Him

Spent time between service and work period in bed reading.

Cooked lunch: German apple pancake, red cabbage salad, creamy squash soup.

House meeting spent monitoring my own internal state. Don tried to say that "abiding in nonintimacy" meant we didn't have to be aware of each other, which bothered me enough that I said, "I can't explicate the sutras in this meeting. But that's not what it means." They also wanted to decide that our problems weren't a fit topic. I said I thought we were expanding the frequency of these meetings and their agenda because the emotional and structural life of this community was problematic.

Long talk with Julie.

Her

Bad night with Isabel—she is up twice, just screaming. I yell at her; she sobs. I am furious. She is in complete tantrum and hysterics mode. It's exhausting. Even Isabel says: "When I yell at you I get tired."

Go to the museum: Rebecca Salsbury James. 1891–1968. Married to Paul Strand. Did she kill herself, at the end? Painting on glass. Lived in Taos. Colcha embroidery. Portrait by Nicolai Fechin. Crippled by arthritis. Her collection of nudes by other people. Something is bothering me here. A tiny black O'Keeffe of Lake George, presumably at night. *The Calla Lily* and *The Rosebud,* reverse oil on glass. "What to say with a tiny stitch…the things I have loved come into the room.…" Earth and water. A shell in the desert. White conch shell and mesa. Tiny milkweed

173

pod on blue, framed in gold. Walking Woman, Taos, New Mexico. Figure in black follows narrow path home, isolated adobe beneath black mountains. "A walking woman, a waiting woman, a mourning woman, a devout woman, cedar posts, old dry wood."

Him

Overcast.

Dreamed Don was wearing white noise generators over his ears so he wouldn't have to hear me.

Lunch cook: macaroni and cheese, buttered parsnips, romaine salad.

Finished Sue Grafton novel, Richard Lupoff, reading *Wild Cards,* a "mosaic" science fiction thing with several authors.

Been doshi mornings, with Mark as doan, and doan evenings.

3.27.92 DATE Angel spaced out while cutting Russell's hair and finally had to shave his head to fix it.

Miriam called, upset, saying, "I have bad news," and I thought, Philip is dead. Isabel is in the hospital. "Susannah is going to need surgery—she has another ectopic," and I was relieved.

Gisela's back from accompanying her friend to chemotherapy in Denver. "I helped her with her diet. No cramps: miso and seaweed."

Rain.

Angel came in for a bit after dinner and asked how I was doing. Told her that, at each tiny incident, instead of thinking, "Oh God, I'm going to be stuck with this bullshit for the rest of my life," I think, "I'm FREE!"

Randy is back, and insists I do the service tomorrow so he can see how it's done.

Her

Susannah has an ectopic pregnancy—surgery—the tube had ruptured. Depression.

Before this happened, a pleasant day like any other. Breakfast with Annie Baylor on Canyon Road, laughing at the guy who spray-painted new city yellow curb lines all over the sidewalk, untidily.

See *Robin Hood, Prince of Thieves*—it is a bit violent, but we love it.

Apricot blossoms.

Hail.

Laundry.

3.27.92
DATE

Him

Woke during han, washed and dressed in a hurry—fortunately I'm still doshi. Came in at the end.

Powdering of frost on the ground. Snow in earnest after breakfast.

Sexual fantasies about Barbara, whom I haven't seen in years. You'd think I'd have had my fill, but it doesn't seem to work that way.

Happy to be free, but disgusted and angry underneath. Each little thing indicates pathology to me, and I have to keep pulling back pulling back. Thus my great desire to be quit of ino-hood. Strong feeling of waiting. Not "doing my time," as Russell said, just waiting in place.

Gisela adjusts the curtains in the zendo—the ino's job. It's her home, her community, and it's hard to cross her. If it were more a *sangha* (a practice comunity), it'd be easier to make the distinctions less personal. Gerald and Gisela take off from evening zazen to spend time together—when they return they sit together in "their" corner of the zendo.

3.28.92
DATE

Dennis's tenure here seems to depend on whether people like him, not on their ability to practice with him. Beata and Lynne roll their eyes at each other while he talks.

Made lunch: Scandinavian hot apple soup, potato kugel, salad.

Randy told tales of Palenque.

Took Russell's car in the afternoon, returned library books, then came back along the northern edge of the valley. Big sky overcast, rain cloud touching down only over Crestone.

Isabel says she misses me, tells the plot of the Costner *Robin Hood,* which seems to be about the rescue of small boys, says an abrupt good-bye, and hangs up.

Skipped evening zazen and read several more Grafton mysteries.

Her

Susannah sounds strong on the phone. My parents arrive from Rome. By prearranged planning, Rachel tells the news, then calls Susannah. My mother says, "Do you think the doctor is *good*?" I say, "I can't even discuss this kind of question."

Paint and draw with Isabel. Sparkles on glue. She watches Frog Prince, I do an hour's desk work. Reading *Palace Walk*. Go to Children's Museum with Isabel and Kath. Then Isabel naps.

Violet and green, the colors you see with your eyes closed, what does it mean to have a family name. Robert asks why I don't write poems in this book.

3.28.92
DATE

Him

Shikunichi.

Randy is doshi, finally.

Dream: I'm arranging flowers in a circle in a flat bowl full of earth on a table, around which a bunch of Zen students and Baker-roshi are sitting. The flowers aren't quite evenly spaced. Roshi wants to know why two are clumped together. I answer. He wants to know if they're sports. I give a conditional answer. He says, "David would know for sure. He's the expert. He should be the one doing this," and I put down the flowers and say, "He should do it then. That was rude. I quit." Roshi acts like he can't imagine why I'm angry. The students act like I'm wrong to be angry.

Gerald's in bed with a busted knee. Gisela isn't in the zendo either.

What I'd thought was the whine of water pipes in the morning is a high-pitched, resonant bell from Mark and Lynne next door.

3.29.92
DATE
Sewed Russell's rakusu with him.

Smoked some of Angel's "schmoogies" with her in Ulrike's room while she ragged on Roshi. Sat outside Beata's room with the two of them, and Angel smoked while I finished her wine. It began to hail just as I was musing about how balmy it was for this cold valley in March. We stayed out in the hail for a while, then moved into Beata's room and got some beers out of the walk-in. Angel continued to rail in an oddly theoretical way. Her father's been taken off chemo; there's nothing more they can do for him. Issan lasted four days from that point. His mother, her grandmother, is still alive, and we talked about how hard that must be, to survive your children. Angel says especially for the Italians and the Jews. Beata says her daughter was born with a hole in her heart, and they thought she wouldn't survive either that or an

178

operation, which the kid finally had at eleven months. "You can't imagine that a baby could die."

Angel and Steve are leaving in a couple days; going to California to see her father. She'll visit Naropa Institute first to see about acupuncture school there—they give a tuition break to Buddhist priests.

Angel came in my room about 10:30, drunk, and repeatedly apologized for what she'd been saying about Roshi. I hadn't cared, and told her so.

Her

Ended up getting depressed about Susannah, and had a hard time shaking it. Took Isabel to the mall and carousel. Lunch at X. and Y.'s lifted my spirits, but their family scene has a feeling of stuck sadness.

3.29.92
DATE

Him

Lay in bed after breakfast. I hear Gisela in the hall asking if I'm sick in a hard voice.

Foggy outside, mysterious and a little depressing. I like the wet twilight, rare here.

Steve came by and we talked about what I intend to do. Small things. Sit fall sesshin here, though I'm not announcing it. Visit some teachers. Spend time with Philip. Steve suggests that I do something formal. I suspect he thinks I should be Phil's student. I'm not sure. We'll see. Dokusan would be about right.

Dream: covered with ticks that are posturing like scorpions. (Too much coffee.)

3.30.92
DATE

Her

More rain. Fun coffee date with Sabrina, who was adorable. Taught an AIDS group in the evening—pretty good—nice to see Mark. Corinna baby-sat, and Isabel is behaving better. Finished videos of *Camelot* and *Hair*.

Him

Shikunichi schedule because we're preparing for sesshin.

Took the table out of my room and set up beds for Tim and Charles, who haven't arrived yet.

Listening to *Metal Man Has Hornet's Wings,* the Zappa-Beefheart bootleg.

Set out POA library books to be returned, wrote last few letters, returned Mom's call. She wanted to tell me a painting of hers I'd wanted, *Midwest Storm* (big abstract, storm over TV), was going into a show, and should she mark it sold and sell it to me on time, or should she sell it. "I might never give it to you anyway." Once we'd negotiated buying it and hung up I realized she'd sold me a painting she'd already given me, and never delivered.

I'm over the hump before sesshin—a couple days in advance I always want OUT, try to think of a way, then it's all right. The first few days I spend breaking down, then, wilted, I continue with some ease, thinking, "This is how man was meant to live." Every time.

3.31.92
DATE

Overcast and snow. Every sesshin here is in snow, September-April.

Read a translation of some Chinese monastic rules that sounded familiar. Many small left-to-right inversions. Miriam and Russell both said it was because they're on the other hemisphere. They pointed the used end of their chopsticks to the right, toward the junior monks. Bathing sounds to have been more about purity than cleanliness, like the Hindus, or a mikva; water poured without removing your underclothes.

Dream about Nazis.

Angel went off the road on the way back from Boulder. Gregory is convinced Steve had predicted it at lunch. We were talking about what a lousy driver she is.

Gregory, who owns a bookstore, asks for a list of my half-dozen favorite books:

Naked Lunch
Howl
Technicians of the Sacred (ed. Rothenberg)
Moby Dick
Huckleberry Finn
Walden
Silence (Cage)

Miriam sounded tired on the phone. She sounds like she thinks she's stressed. When she's really stressed she's meaner, snappier. When she's anticipating future stress she sounds tired and worried. It'll be our tenth anniversary in October, and we might go to Atlantic City, leaving Isabel with the grandparents.

3.31.92 DATE

Don, Mark, and Randy performed the sesshin orientation, while I wished myself elsewhere. Don: "The body rebels, but the spirit rejoices," what nonsense; part of a speech about all monastic traditions having common threads and other perennial theology. Somehow they've dropped the actual sesshin admonitions, specific and weighty, in favor of panegyrics and conservation tips, mentioning repeatedly how "weird" sesshin is. Aggggg!

Her

Rain in the morning. I haven't managed to do one nice thing a day as I'd promised myself. It fell apart when Susannah got sick.

I did buy a great Virgin of Guadalupe T-shirt at Mira's yesterday, and admire all the items, including Frida Kahlo fetishes/altars. Who is making these? What are the secret cults of the ladies of Santa Fe?

Edit femmes—good group.

Tuesday club takes Reuben and Isabel to the mall for carousel, fountains, jelly beans, popcorn, and pet store. They both go to sleep at 6 P.M.

3.31.92
DATE

Him

Many angry thoughts. Sore knee.

You have no eyes
Only ears to hear
In the heavy water
Like blackout, NYC
Doorway conversation
Right in your face
The pool under your sleep
Is calling, banks
Tilting toward it

Her

A good day. Morning to myself. Dance around the house to Bruce Springsteen, and finally cry about Susannah. Many errands. Joan comes to dinner and we dash out to Renée's reading, a festive literary event, with networking and raspberry soda.

Him

Impatient.

Sesshin jukebox.

Sounds of exercise or sex through the wall from Beata's room rising in pitch at the end. Glimpse of her in the hall looking dark and smelling of cigarettes, waiting for the bathroom.

Her

Buy three cute outfits at K-Mart—shorts and miniskirt.

Take Isabel for a haircut.

Snow and rain.

Angel and Steve arrive, sushi dinner. Steve spends a long time looking at my astrological chart on his little computer, Isabel's too. Her moon is in Cancer. The stars that mark your body, a birthmark in the shape of Nebraska, a liver shaped like the Andromeda galaxy.

4.2.92
DATE

The old lady, right-hand neighbor, crosses my house on her way back from her daughter's, the left-hand neighbor. Early morning, she wears a coat over her housedress, slippers, carries a cup full of lard. It's about to snow. The apricot blossoms will freeze, she tells me. I can tell she loves the tree on her side of the wall. I love it too. She inquires after Isabel, now three. "Time passes," she says, "time passes."

Him

Strawberry kefir.

Roshi:
"Put your mind in your hands."
"Putting death in the stream of your life."

"The moon outside my window
is always different
Or is it me?
The moon is in my nostril
Have you asked for instruction?"

4.3.92
DATE

186

Her

Wake up early. Sunshine. Cold. Forsythia.

Steve and Angel are still here, fixing the car that got smashed up when Angel went off a 10-foot embankment at the top of the San Luis Valley.

I feel as if a great weight of fatigue is lifting from me, but slowly. This whole stint, these three months, finally exhausted me—the commute, monastery, Zen crises, single motherhood, finally Susannah's ectopic and surgery.

Isabel a bit pesky, but all right. I've been tougher on her. Her inherent sweet nature shines through. She asked me in the car at great length about death: "Are you very old? Are you going to die soon? My animals (stuffed) aren't going to die."

I wish Robert were here, although I slightly dread his reentry.

Sharon took me out for a nice breakfast, on the paper. Assigned me an article. I have a new one for *Sage,* too. My editing night class is pretty much full. Still need two to four students for Thursday. Almost two weeks left.

Woke up this morning, thinking a dread thought: I need leisure to write poetry. A bad dream about trying to write, being in school, my mother.

Him

Someone picks up the telephone and slams it down. Listening in. Just when I'd convinced myself they're not that hateful. Still angry. Nearly continuous but muted. Miriam says, "Work out your salvation with diligence."

Dream: saying "Stay!" returns melting flesh to woman's face. Temporarily.

Roshi: "Living in a monastery is much more important than being a priest."

Are mysteries paranoid?

Jolt up my spine and vertigo when Roshi was sitting near.

Roshi squeezes my hand when I bring hot water.

Coffee.

4.4.92
DATE

Her

Such a cold spring.

Do a load of whites. Dry on the inside rack, threat of rain.

Steve and Angel leave for California.

Take Isabel to the Folk Art Museum for Creepy Crawlers movies and bug making.

Car wash. Much needed.

Watching *Singing in the Rain*.

Actual rain.

Some depression all day, seemingly without cause, can't find the right level of stimulation or activity.

I miss Robert more than I admit to myself. Getting enough done, on a small task-oriented level, but the picture seems obscure on the larger, as if I see myself, tiny from a distance.

A feeling that I have accomplished nothing, and never will, but what…

Him

Vile retread. Mechanical crickets.
Finally, bliss kicks in.

Her

Birthday party for Maggie at the Children's Museum—a great success.

4.5.92
DATE

Kath comes by. Take Isabel for a walk.
Get my period.

Him

Roshi changed a detail of the oryoki yesterday, stopping the meal and lecturing in the zendo: put the *setsu* (cleaning stick) in the large bowl and bow with the water, except in the evening, when you hold the setsu beside the bowl (because you're using a smaller bowl). Today I remembered why we dropped that bit, a year or three ago: because Roshi asked us to.

Dream: welded spring around the bottom of the teakettle falls off—amusing. "The bottom falling out of the bowl" is an enlightenment trope.

Flecks of brown paint from the floor have glued themselves to the insides of my sandals.

Nodding out in zazen. Series of images leads to: Isabel's head in the mailbox. Jerk awake, fervently let it pass.

4.6.92
DATE

Her

Mood lifts with blood flow.
Sabrina comes over with a pretty wand and crown for Isabel.

Him

Dokusan with Roshi.

Visualizing Mir in a variety of pleasantly obscene positions generates a sexual charge I can ram up my spine to stay awake in zazen. Lasts about ten minutes of clear, buzzed out, imageless zazen.

Up late after sesshin talking to Tim, who's assistant curator of the botany museum at Boulder. All these Gary Snyder fans are ectomorphs.

Her

Feel well rested. Feel more in sync with Isabel. I get it: she is not me.

Lovely Tuesday club date with Hope and Reuben. Walk from Hope's house to the Fenn Gallery, sculpture, ducks. The kids love it. Reuben says the elephant fountain is peeing.

4.7.92
DATE

Him

Shikunichi schedule.

Beets from lunch borscht yesterday finally appeared red in the toilet—twenty-two hours. Digestion slows way down during sesshin.

Buddha's birthday. Procession with *inkins* (handled bells with brocade cloths). The high inkin leads, Roshi bangs his staff, flower petals tossed by an embarrassed Olaf, clappers gingerly struck by Lynne, the lower inkin by me. Russell says the interval between the two is a chickadee's two-note call reversed.

Talked with Roshi before we left and hugged good-bye.

Don: "I could see you had a hard time in sesshin. I thought you were going to leave several times." I thanked him, but couldn't imagine what he was talking about, unless it was pure projection.

Russell and I stopped to watch a herd of elk in Carson National Forest on the way home.

4.8.92
DATE

Multiple greetings with Miriam and Isabel.

Her

Strange anxiety all day. Warm. Haze of apricot blossoms. Christina works on my hip. Walk with Isabel. Rough draft two articles. My taxes are okay—big overpayment, budget stable. Nothing helps. Need two more students.

Robert comes home 8 P.M.-ish. Immediately I feel fine, just fine, as if I have unconsciously been listening for burglars for three months and have just stopped. Isabel is ecstatic. After she goes to sleep we have great sex. Isabel wets her diaper, crawls into our bed around 5:30 A.M., but pretty good, as she'd virtually been sleeping with me with Robert gone.

Him

Woke at four, then slept to eight.

Happily bicycling around town—bought magazines at Downtown Subscription, chatting with the lady there; left off some of Suzi's *Fish Drum* issue. Went to the library.

Picked up Isabel at day care and walked the bike home with her on my shoulders, loudly telling "Jack and the Beanstalk." Sunburned my head a little.

Raked the backyard, started spring cleaning the house.

Left Isabel at Hope and Greg's and went to eat sushi dinner with Miriam.

Sat on their lawn with the kids at dusk.

Her

Warm. Robert playing rock and roll: John Fogerty, Patti Smith, Rolling Stones, Springsteen's "Jersey Girl." It makes me feel I can read his mind. Feels great to all be under our own roof, even if the floorboards are rotting out under the washing machine.

What do I want. Something is off. All yesterday I felt I had wasted my life, being a poet. And what do I know. And what do I know how to do. I kept thinking: I should get a stable job and go work for the post office. At Dave's, where Isabel and I went for a lemonade, the waitress said: you're the writer. I want something but not just another gig. I'm thirty-eight years old. In my pink flip-flops and spandex pants I just look like another Mafia mother from New Jersey dropping her kid off at school.

Him

Breakfast conference with supervisor Andy at the Burrito Co. Not only do I have my old job back, but I have the same hours, despite changes at the library.

More *Fish Drum* to Caxton's, where Jean said she was glad I was back.

Called Brian and Tom. Saw posters for Brian's band and "Beat Happening" show tonight. Ran into Miriam on my way to the Aztec. Wandering.

Apricot trees are blooming white perfume all over town.

Explained to Isabel about bees and flowers and honey.

Julie's present to her is a walking gorilla. Isabel fled, then kissed it on the nose and said she loved it.

Found the kind of industrial-grade thongs we used to carry at the Zen Center grocery that Julie wanted. The dilemma is, they're carried in a catalog of someone involved in the Zen Central breakup and exile to Santa Fe. I decided that Jews traditionally have been willing to trade with the enemy, and to please Julie. Have to find her shoe size.

4.10.92
DATE

Isabel: "We're going to make a fire in the fireplace. The kind of fire that won't come near us because it's made of glass. A glass fire."

Isabel: "Fee fi bumblebee."

Her

Last day of the diary.
What have I left out.
Spring.
The floor beneath our washing machine is rotted away. Laundry.
Things that give me unmixed pleasure: buying clothes, eating sushi.
I think every mole I have is cancer.
It's spring.
Robert cleans the yard.
I love Robert.
I love Isabel.
I love my yellow shirt.
It's spring.
Robert turns on the sprinkler and wets my otherwise dry laundry.
Yellow tulips in the backyard.
Boxes of novels in the bedroom.
The usual confusion.
I grew to like the commute, but never the monastery.
Feel as if I am emerging from a narrow space.
Anyway, it's spring.

4.10.92
DATE

Afterword

I met Robert and Miriam in 1986 at Cerro Gordo Temple in Santa Fe after one of Richard Baker-roshi's Sunday lectures. No sooner did I begin to sit there in the mornings than I was under investigation. "If you're here for more than a week," said Robert, "we're going to know everything about you." The first time I visited their home on Santa Fe Avenue, Miriam observed: "Tom, you have inky fingers. You must be a writer."

Robert says in *Dirty Laundry*: "I can't figure out...why Zen students who ostensibly accept the interpenetration of all things are obsessed with purity." His laughter, and the laughter he provoked in others, was the antidote to our puritanical disease. One time, when Baker-roshi was sick, Robert made him some chicken soup. Reprimanded for cooking a chicken, Robert protested, "But it was dead when I found it!"

He was a wise guy, and he took the exercise of his particular brand of wisdom as a serious vocation, one in no way inferior to or separate from the vocation of being a priest. It sometimes got him into trouble. He belongs to the lineage of foolish monks who don't fit in with the program, whose eccentricities confront us, often uncomfortably, with our ideas of perfection.

Robert and Miriam, as teachers, and I, as a student, attended a writing retreat with Natalie Goldberg at Hokyo-ji, Katagiri-roshi's retreat center in Iowa. I remember writhing (that's *writhing*) on the grass with back spasms while the participants chanted an Allen Ginsberg poem in the zendo; and, at the end of the retreat, Robert's dedication, in the presence of Miriam and the whole world, to "all my lovers, past, present, and future."

Before Hokyo-ji, it had never occurred to me that you could write with other people. Writing had to be done in dreadful seclusion, didn't it? Robert and I made a pact to meet once a week, if possible, and write together. We did meet—usually at the Downtown Subscription, when it was still downtown—and for years we actually wrote. He was reliably fifteen or thirty minutes late. A connoisseur of trash literature, before sitting down to write he had to look at all the trashy magazines, and he usually bought two or three. From the start, there was a feeling between us that we could not wrong one another, although it almost wore thin the time he stood me up for our writing date and I left a message on his answering machine pretending to be "Louise," I think it was, and saying in a betrayed woman's voice, "I waited and waited, and you never came. You can't treat me like this. Don't bother calling me anymore." Miriam took the message, and for once, Robert was at a loss for words.

Eventually we moved to the new Downtown Subscription, where we did a lot more talking than writing. The inexhaustible subjects of conversation were the Zen community, books, and love. He talked me through two major relationships and suggested others. For himself, he confessed, "I like being married," which mostly had to do with Miriam and Isabel, but also with his discovery that women were less guarded with a married man: it was easier to know them as friends. Gossip was a nourishing function with us, as essential as eating or sitting. After all, Baker-roshi was always citing word origins in lecture, and didn't *gossip* and *gospel* have the same linguistic root?

He was the career Zen man, I the devoted layperson, although the distinction never counted for much between us. When I bellyached about my lack of ambition in "the Zen biz," as he called it, he said, "So what? You just want to sit, right?"

For himself, both before and after the Practice Period from Hell, he struggled to understand what his vocation entailed. Baker-roshi told him, "Take care of Miriam and Isabel." Did that mean backing off from monk's practice? As he became weaker, questions of how to practice, or with whom, resolved themselves into questions of whether or not he was going to be able to practice at all. His head newly shaved, deathly pale in his black robes and in a mopping sweat from his medications, he gave a formal lecture at the temple to a religion class from the College of Santa Fe. Twice, I drove him to Mountain Cloud Zen Center to hear Father Pat Hawk-roshi talk during sesshin. He missed being in the zendo the same way he missed clambering around out of doors in the light and air.

When it came to writing, Robert chided me the way Baker-roshi chided him. He pried me loose from a book manuscript and sent it off to be published. He demanded pieces for his literary magazine *Fish Drum*. For the rest of his life, he nagged me to write about the peyote church, which I had been involved in during the 1970s. ("I'm not a bird in a cage," I told him. "I do not sing on command.") Not long before he died, he had me expound on the church at length, over coffee at the Subscription, while he took notes. He was interested in the language that goes along with that religion, and he wanted to steal some of it for song lyrics with his band *Bichos*.

Otherwise, for the last year or so of our writing partnership, we never set pen to paper. For this we forgave each other: it was understood that when we met, writing was, and had always been, beside the point. He talked about his doctors and medications. I talked about my marriage, which I was writing a book about. When it came time for me to leave the family and move into the temple, Robert characteristically saw it as a successful conclusion to the book, rather than an unsuccessful end to the marriage. Throughout its pages, and in my life without him, he keeps me from taking things too seriously.

Tom Ireland
Bozburun, Turkey
March 1997

Afterword to the New Edition

Dirty Laundry was an idiosyncratic book to write, an odd book to publish. When Robert and I set out to keep our joint diaries of a sojourn at a Zen monastery we had few models; certainly it is more usual for spouses to hide their diaries from one another than to create them together. *Dirty Laundry* had a complex history, for one of its authors died before it was published. When the book came out I was left as the official survivor of a pair, the widow, an author seemingly able to interpret words I hadn't written. It was disconcerting to read aloud from the book at signing parties and hear my own voice recite the not always flattering observations Robert had made about me.

Like all books, *Dirty Laundry* also began to have a life of its own, through its readers. It seemed to serve as a kind of Rorschach. American Zen students obviously read it to find either a mirror or shadow of their own experience. But seekers who had lived on communes, followed gurus, sought community, or experienced conversions found some touchstone here, particularly in the contradictions between the ideals and realities of monastic life. If, as a generation, we were driven to some alternative to the family life we had grown up with, we found some of those negative dynamics re-created even in remote spiritual settings.

Readers were also drawn to the detailed, although almost inadvertent, portrait of a small child at a particular developmental stage. At the time, Robert and I were so immersed in the experience that we assumed Isabel's nightmares and tantrums were caused by the situation, while we also took credit for her verbal leaps and charm. Of course in retrospect she is a textbook example of a three-year-old. When Isabel, at the age of ten, asked if she could read this book, I of course said no. The diaries reveal what parents most wish to hide from their offspring—sex, anger, and insecurity. And yet should she read it as a woman I suspect the thing she will see the most is how her father loved her. His concern for her is obvious on nearly every page.

In this time after the first publication of *Dirty Laundry* what is left most hauntingly is the realization of how difficult it is to tell even a partial truth.

The book, because of its purely confessional nature, creates an assumption that what is written here is real, honest, and accurate. But it is an illusion, nonetheless. We did indeed attempt to tell the truth, albeit a subjective one. But surely if I had kept a record of the next hundred days—a peaceful spring of gardening, working, and a trip to London—the marriage, characters, and concerns would appear completely different. Still, it is just this approximate rawness that gives diaries their power.

Dirty Laundry, as a book, lacks resolution. In the end, not much happened; we went back to daily life. These diaries are not a novel, in which tensions build to be resolved, in which character is clarified by insight, in which the story—for better or worse—is finally over. Indeed, the diaries are like life itself: inherently unresolved. Robert's death gave a finality to his story, but that occurred outside the frame of the book. In a novel, he would have found another teacher, reconciled with his first, or become disillusioned. The issues of the book would be addressed, and solved. In life, of course, none of these things happened in any exact fashion.

Toward the end of *Dirty Laundry* I wrote that I hoped Robert would continue as a formal Zen practitioner, and that I couldn't imagine leading just an "ordinary life." In this I now know I was deluded, although I could not have foreseen the future. Caring for an ill husband, taking care of a child alone, supporting a household—these were extreme states, as were the crises of being widowed. An ordinary life, by comparison, looked like paradise. Today I do indeed lead an ordinary life, a life that includes no monastery, no two-hundred-mile commute, no conflict between family and religious life. Perhaps seeing its beauty, and realizing its transitory nature, was Robert's last gift to me.

Miriam Sagan
Santa Fe, New Mexico
Autumn 1999

About the Authors

Miriam Sagan was born in Manhattan in 1954; **Robert Winson** was born there in 1959. They were both raised in Bergen County, New Jersey, but met in San Francisco in 1981. They were married at San Francisco Zen Center in 1982 and lived in a flat on Rose Alley. In 1984, they moved together to Santa Fe, New Mexico. Their daughter was born in 1989. Robert was ordained as a Zen Buddhist priest in 1990.

Robert was a high school drop-out who studied writing with poet Philip Whalen, sociology at UC-Berkeley, and Buddhism with Richard Baker-roshi. He was a shop steward at the San Francisco Sierra Club, and the pastry manager at Green Gulch Greengrocers. In Santa Fe, he worked for the public library. He was the founder and publisher of the literary magazine *Fish Drum*. He was also the DJ for *Fish Drum on the Air* and *The Third Ear,* a free-form radio show on KLSK at the Santa Fe Community College. In Albuquerque, he led a Buddhist sitting group at Living Batch Bookstore.

Miriam and Robert were the vocals with a punk band, *Poetry Devils*, with Brian Curley. Their work was published in "Performance" from Aural Mural Music in 1990. The self-titled CD caused quite a stir amongst local literati. Robert went on to form his own band, *Bichos*, which played in galleries, cafes, and performance spaces throughout New Mexico. Their CD "Four Legs in the Morning" appeared in 1996.

Miriam Sagan's books include *Aegean Doorway* (Zephyr Press, 1984), *True Body* (Parallax Press, 1991), *Pocahontas Discovers America* (Adastra Press, 1993), *The Art of Love* (La Alameda Press, 1994), and *Unbroken Line: Writing in the Lineage of Poetry* (Sherman Asher, 1999). In 1991, Robert published her chapbook *Advice to the Unborn Baby* with Fish Drum Press. They jointly edited Philip Whalen's *Canoeing Up Cabarga Creek: Buddhist Poems* (Parallax Press, 1996).

Robert died in 1995, at the age of 36. Miriam Sagan lives with her daughter Isabel and her second husband, Richard Feldman, in Santa Fe, New Mexico.

COLOPHON

Set in
MONOTYPE Italian Old Style~
a typeface based on the examples of
15*th* century Venetian printer
Nicolas Jenson.

•

Doves, the brook & vale
a slant of renaissance
savor of cloister
almost golden
ideals

New World Library is dedicated to publishing books, video tapes and audio cassettes that inspire and challenge us to improve the quality of our lives and our world. Our books and tapes are available at bookstores everywhere. For a complete catalog, contact:

New World Library
14 Pamaron Way
Novato, California 94949

Phone: (415) 884-2100
Fax: (415) 884-2199

Or call toll free: (800) 972-6657
Catalog requests: Ext. 50
Ordering: Ext. 52

E-mail: escort@nwlib.com
www.nwlib.com